Beauty of Nature
Reflections and Close Ups

Joanne Guillard

Beauty of Nature Reflections and Close Ups Joanne Guillard

Copyright © 2017 by Joanne Guillard. All rights reserved.
Cover Photo Copyright © Joanne Guillard. All rights reserved.
Photography Copyright © Joanne Guillard. All rights reserved.

Scripture quotations are taken from The Holy Bible, New King James Version.

Copyright © 1982 by Thomas Nelson, Inc. All rights reserved.

ISBN-13: 978-1976816769

ISBN-10: 1976816762

No part of this book may be reproduced in any written, electronic, recording, or photocopying without written permission of the publisher or author. The exception would be in the case of brief quotations embodied in the critical articles or reviews and pages where permission is specifically granted by the publisher or author.

Dedication

To all that need encouragement, to photographers and photography lovers.

As a photographer you have many options of what type of photos you will produce. I was always drawn to nature and landscape photographs. I want my art to reach someone's soul and inspire them to do better and be better.

Contents

Dedication

Contents

Faith

Peace

Healing

Strength

Giving

Trust

Hope

Power

Love

Patience

Milkweed Bug

Bandwing Dragonfly

Zebra Longwing Butterfly

Garden Lizard

Skipper Butterfly

Oleander Caterpillar

Anole Lizard

Golden Silk Spider

Lubber Grasshopper

Curly Tail Lizard

Honeybee

Crab Spider

Monarch Butterfly

Crab Spider

Garden Lizard

Curly tailed Lizard

Skipper Butterfly

Brown Anole Lizard

Hoverfly

Honeybee

Blow Fly

Giant Swallowtail

About the Author

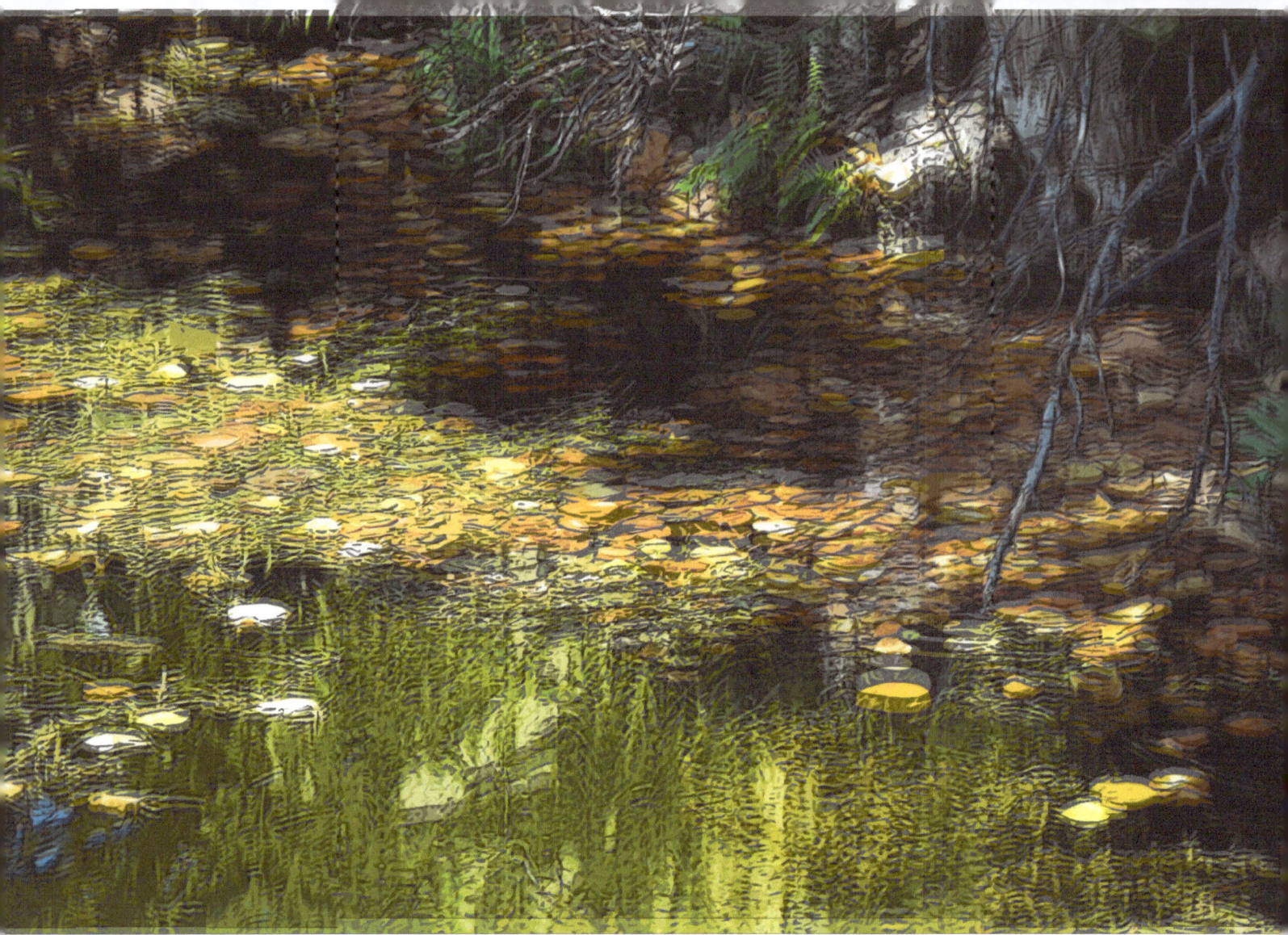

Faith

Now faith is the substance of things hoped for, the evidence of things not seen.
Hebrews 11:1

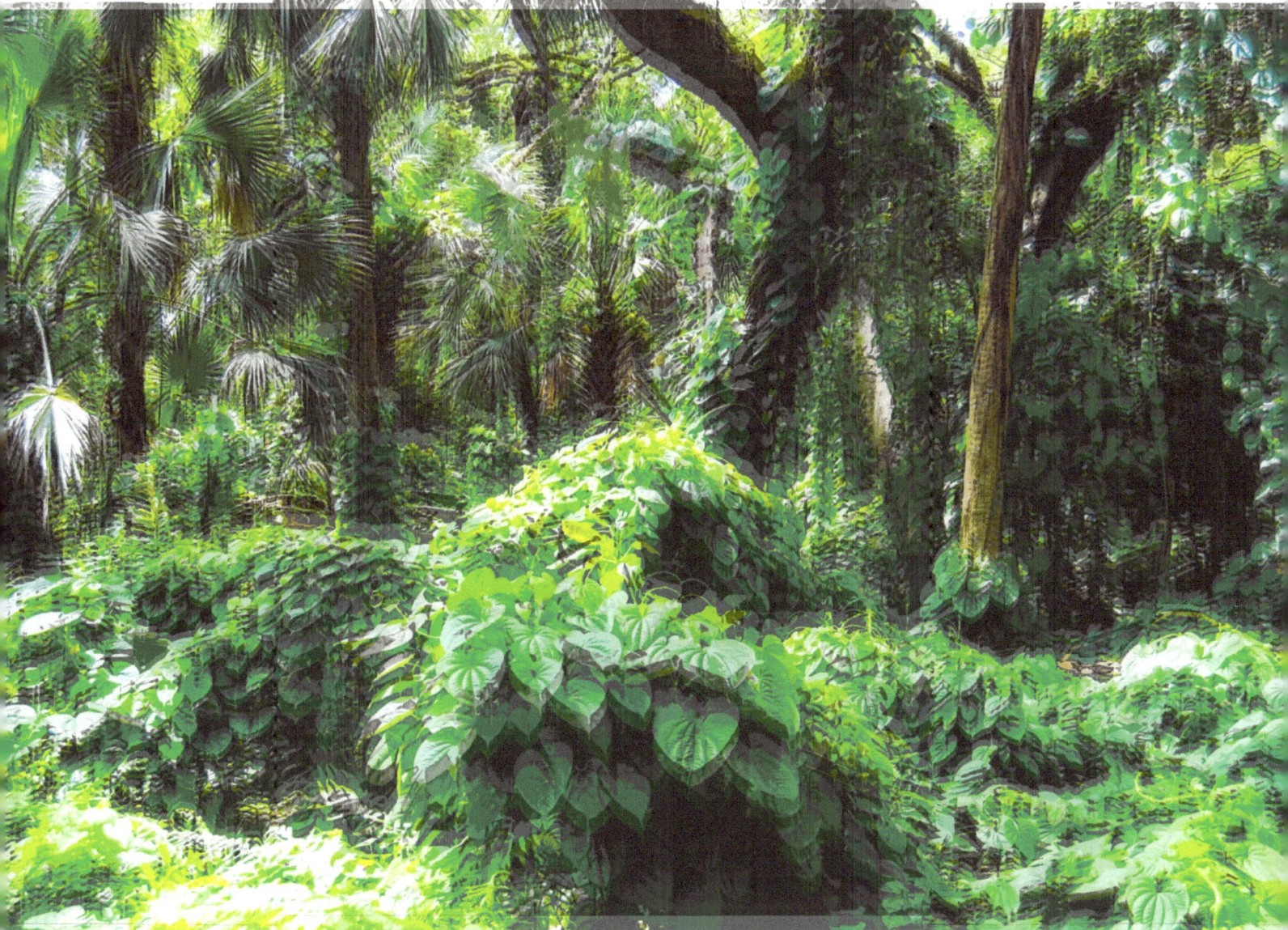

Peace

"Peace I leave with you; My peace I give to you; not as the world gives do I give to you. Let not your heart be troubled, neither let it be afraid."
John 14:27

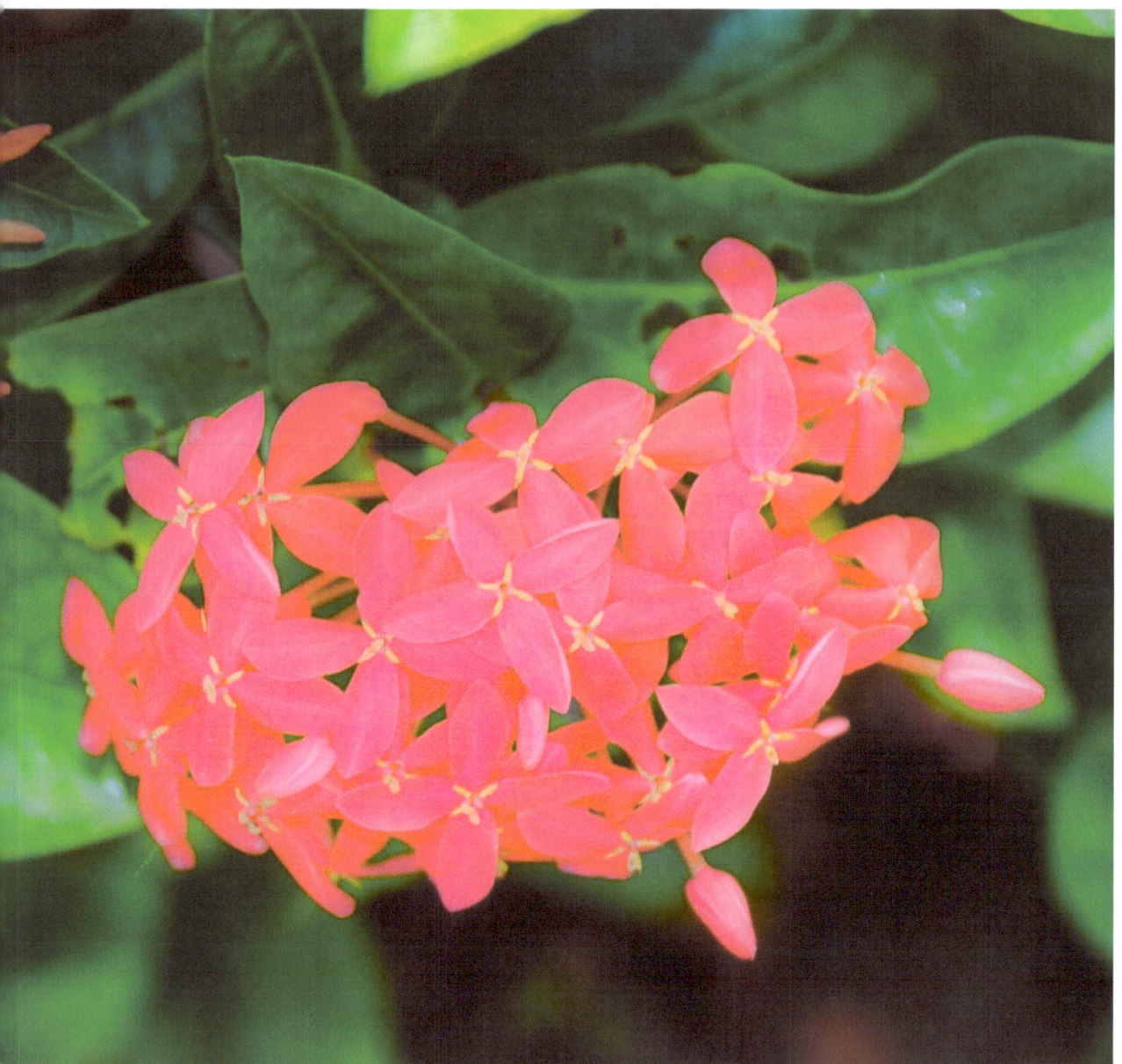

Healing

"Behold, I will bring it health and healing; I will heal them and reveal to them the abundance of peace and truth."
Jeremiah 33:6

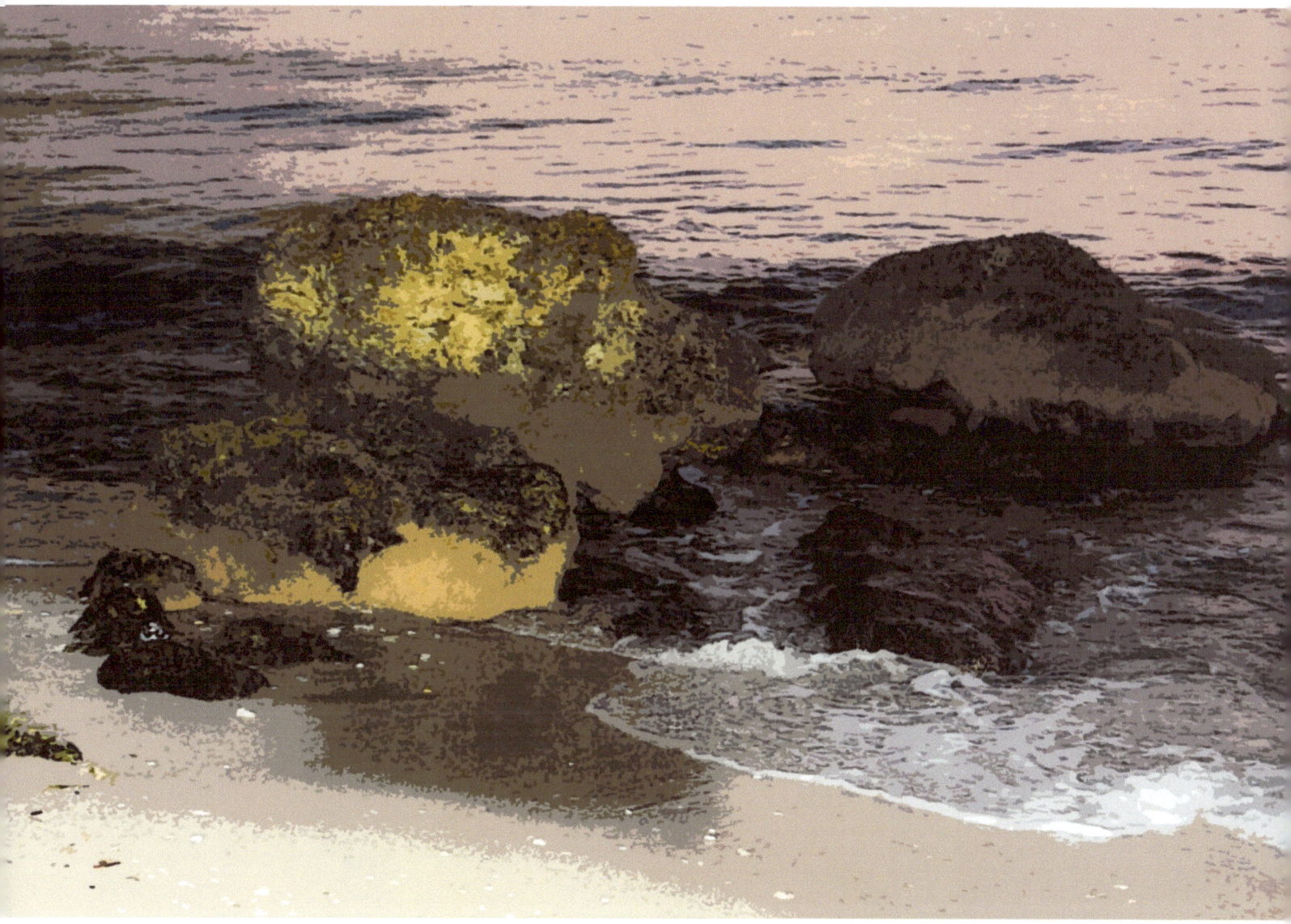

Strength

"The Lord is my strength and song,
And He has become my salvation."
Psalm 118:14

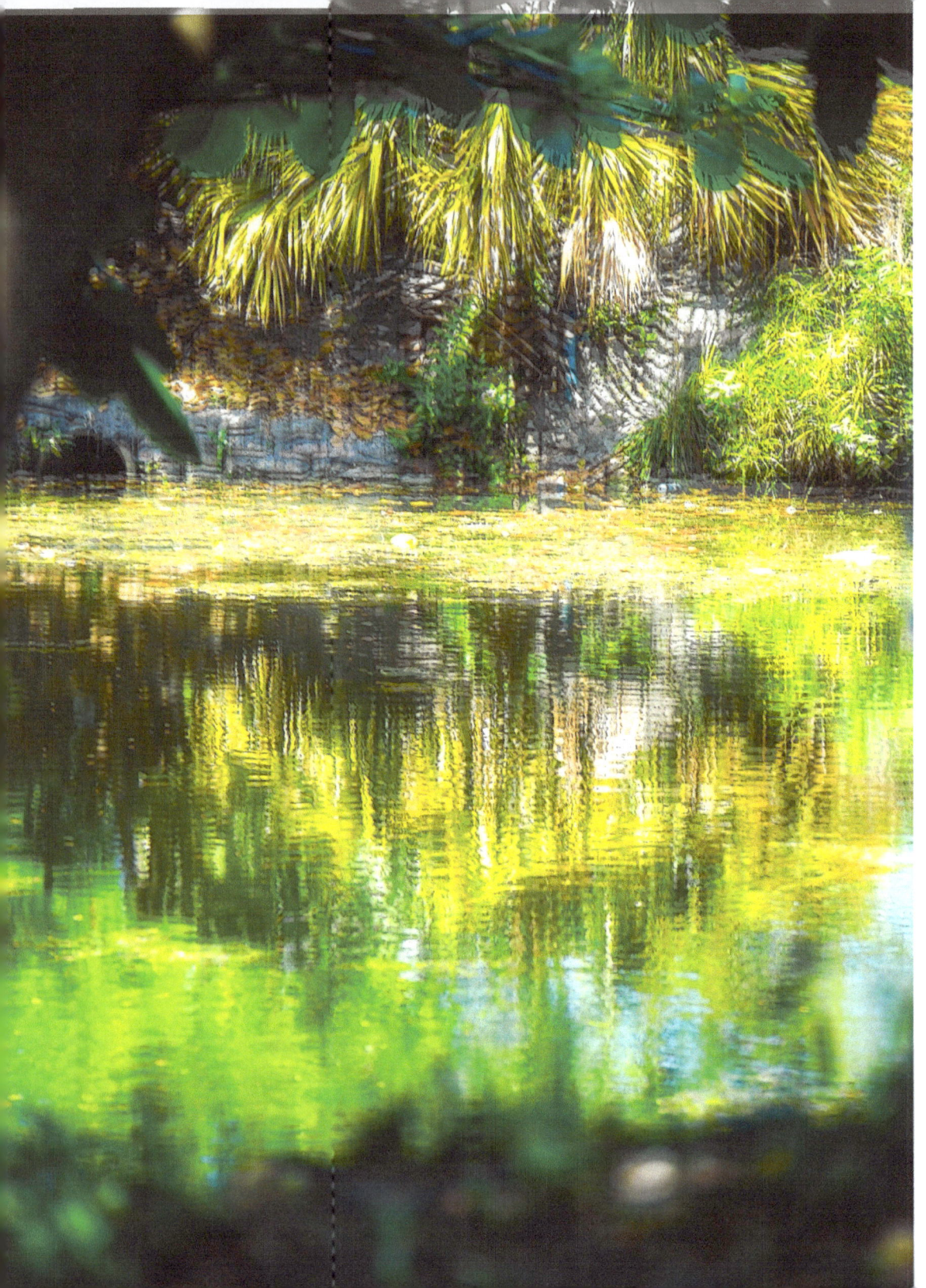

Giving

"Give, and it will be given to you: good measure, pressed down, shaken together, and running over will be put into your bosom. For with the same measure that you use, it will be measured back to you."
Luke 6:38

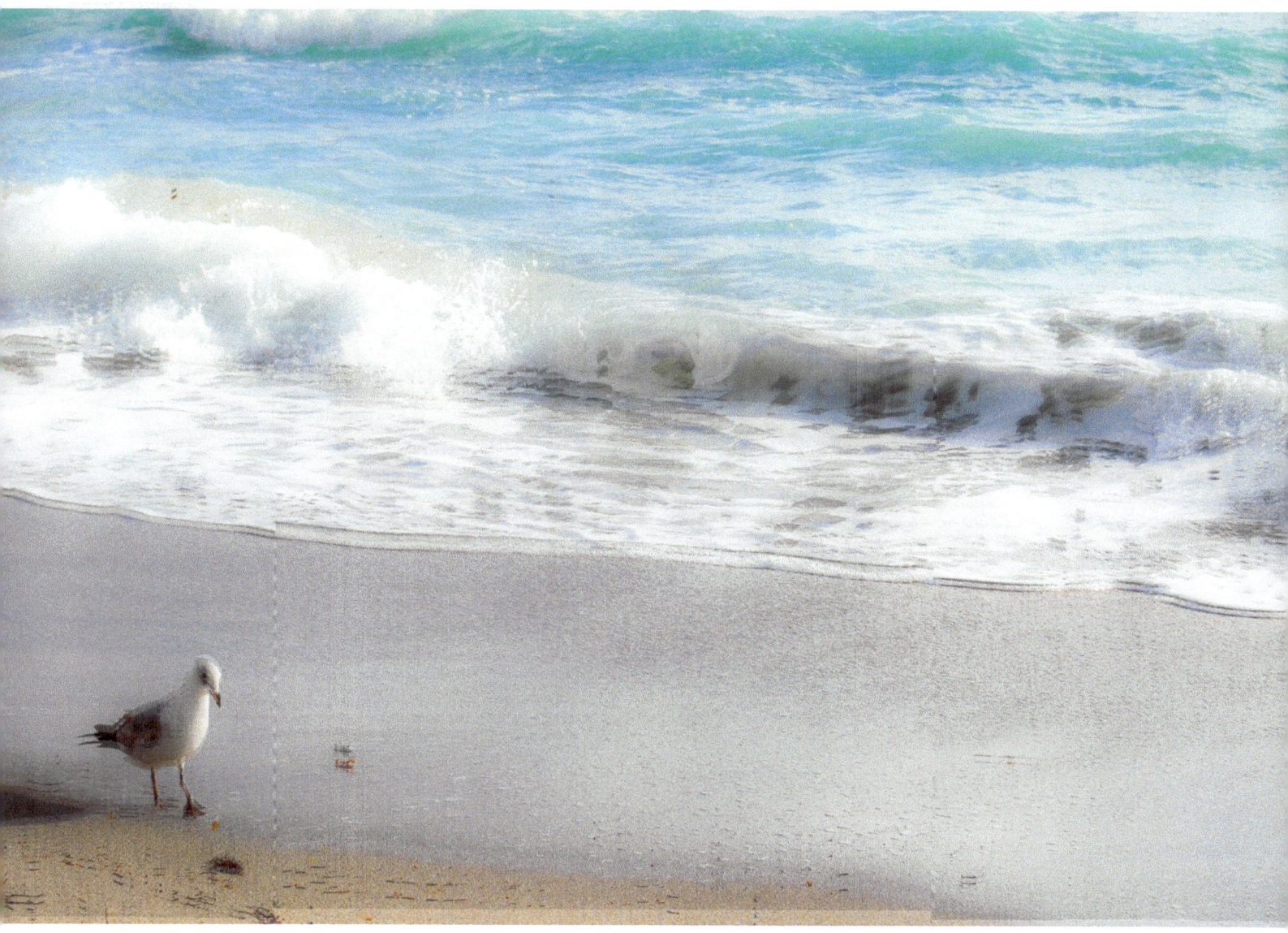

Trust

"Every word of God is pure;
He is a shield to those who put their trust in Him."
Proverbs 30:5

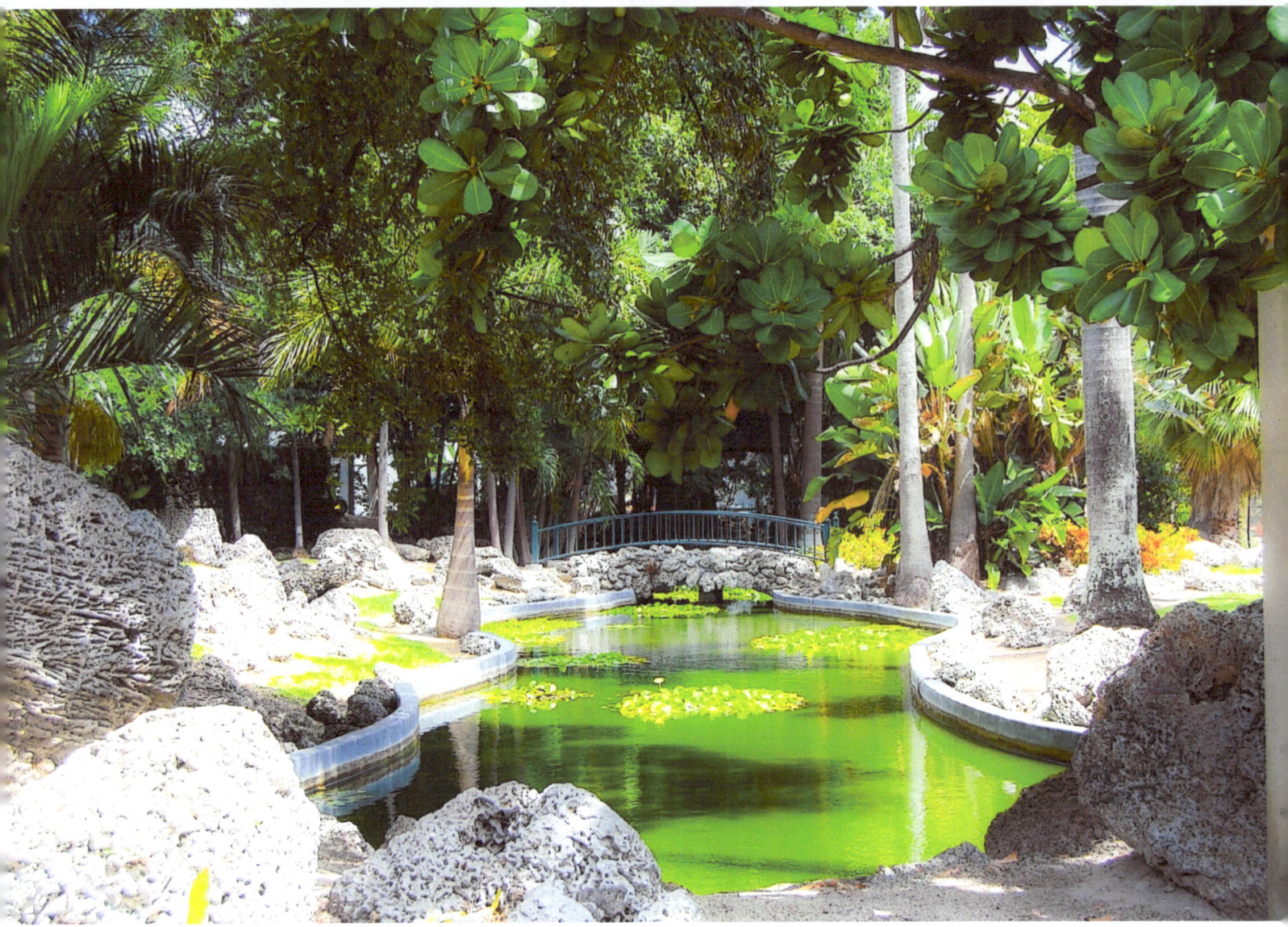

Hope

"rejoicing in hope, patient in tribulation, continuing steadfastly in prayer;"
Romans 12:12

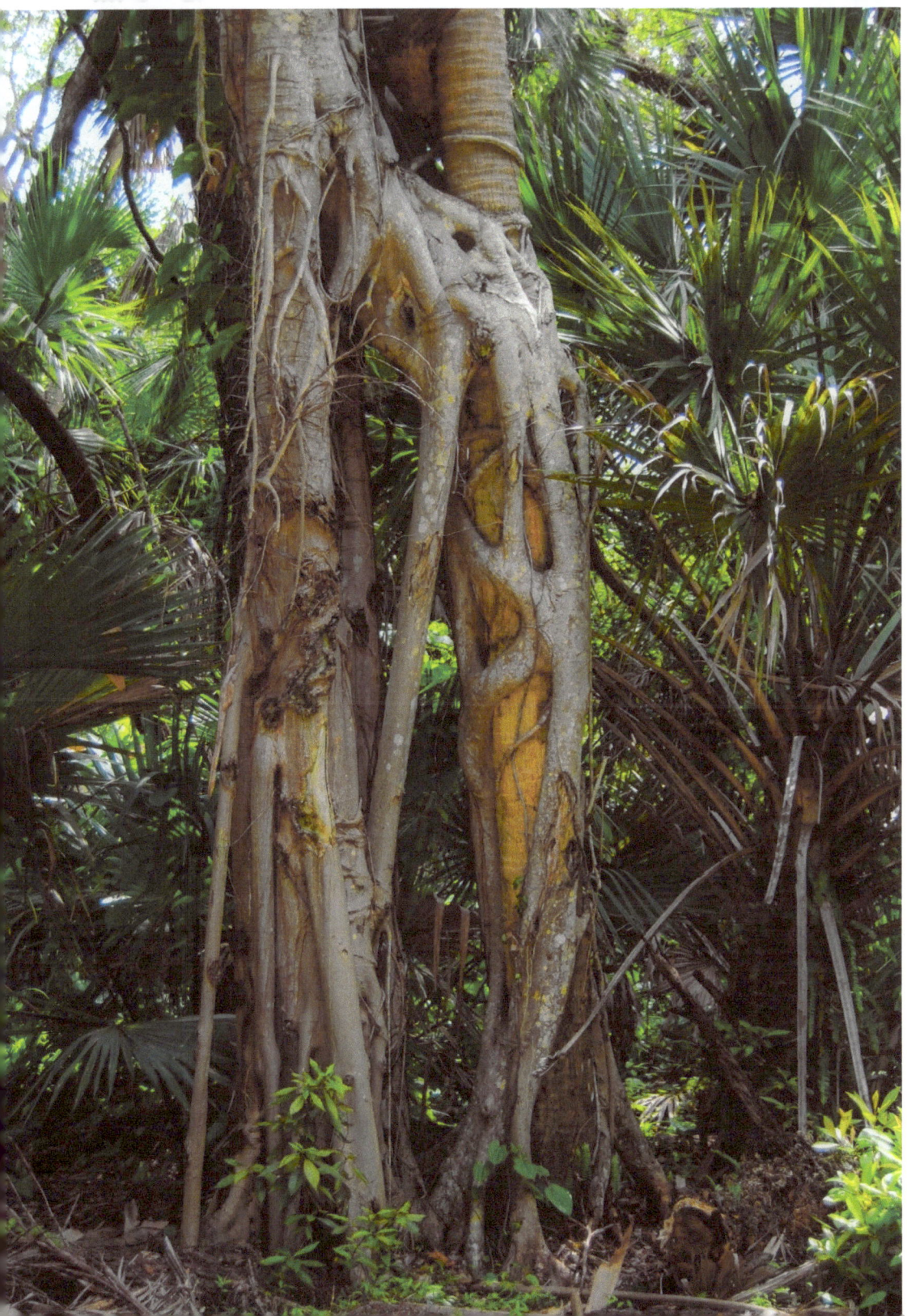

Power

"Now this is the confidence that we have in Him, that if we ask anything according to His will, He hears us."
1 John 5:14

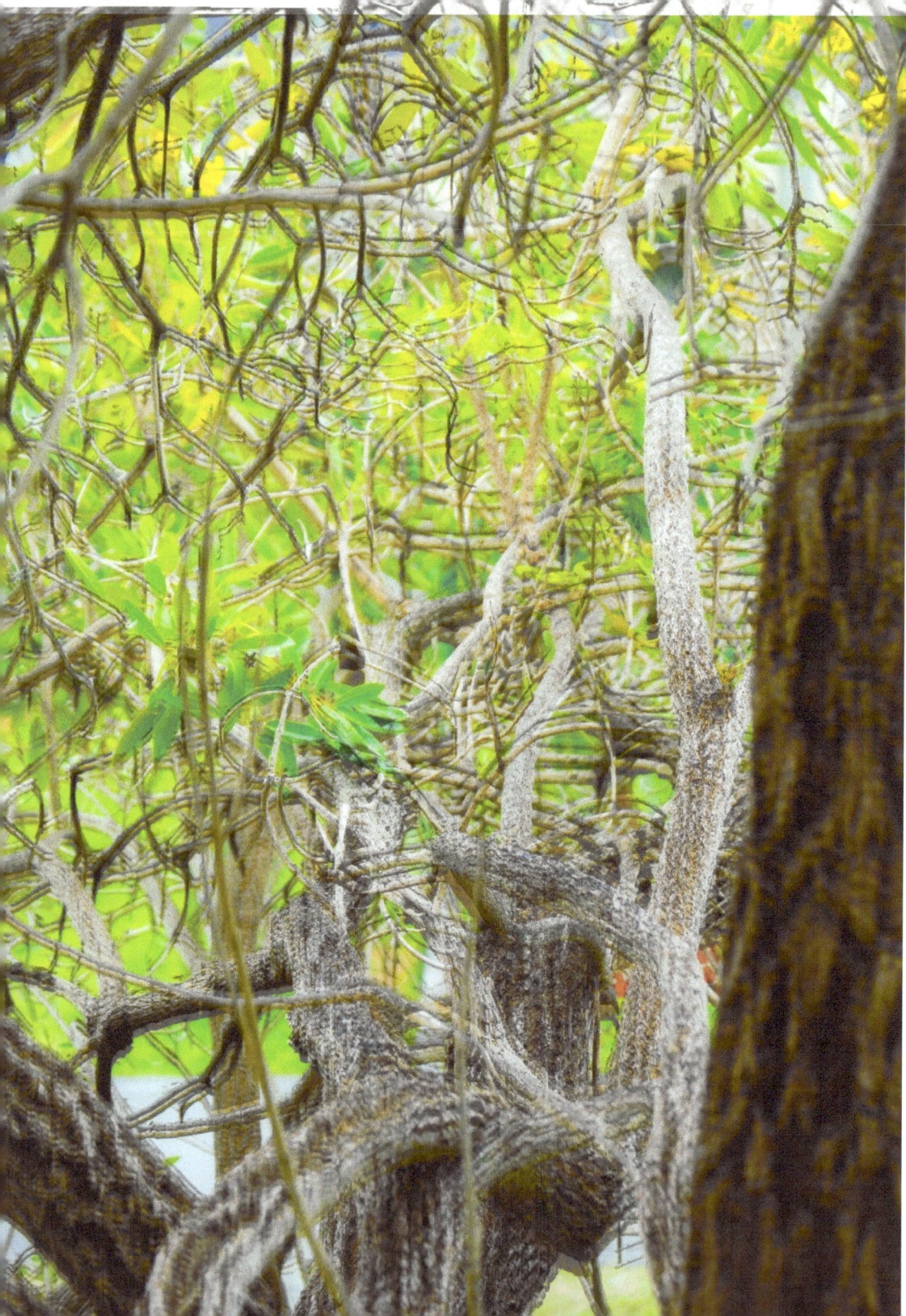

Love

"For God so loved the world that He gave His only begotten Son, that whoever believes in Him should not perish but have everlasting life."
John 3:16

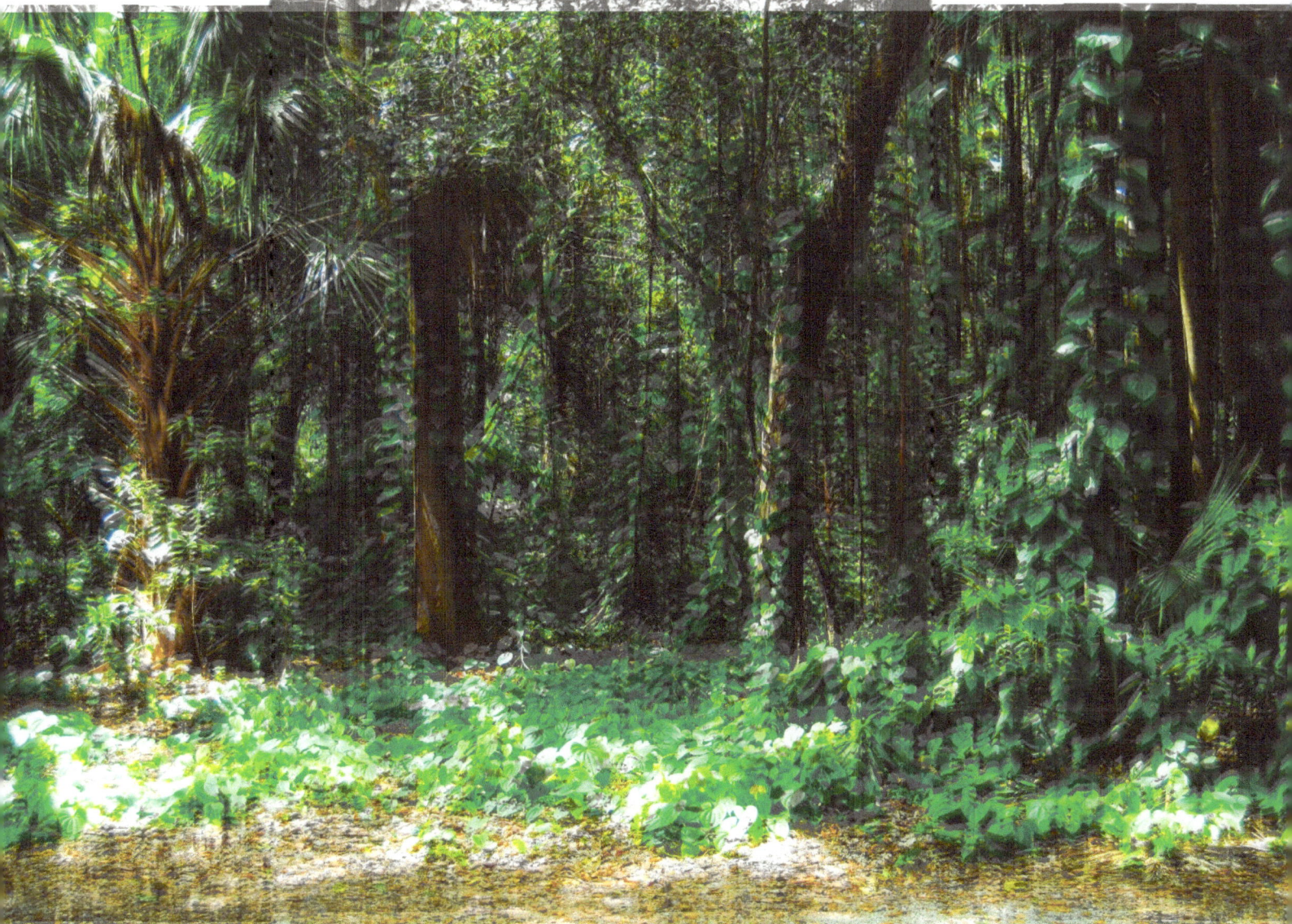

Patience

"Be anxious for nothing, but in everything by prayer and supplication, with thanksgiving, let your requests be made known to God."

Philippians 4:6

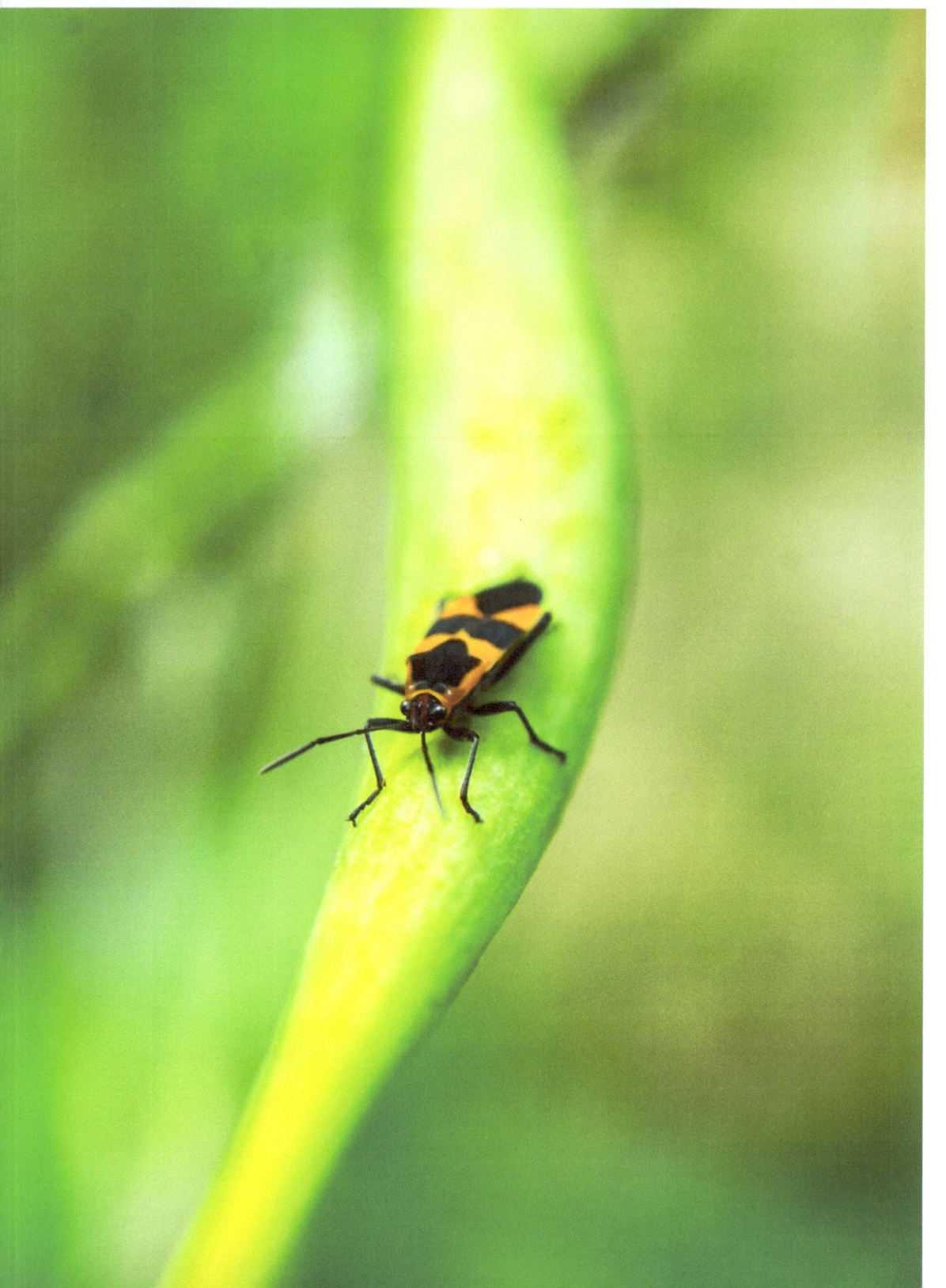

Milkweed Bug
Miami, FL, 2017
Miami Beach
Botanical Garden

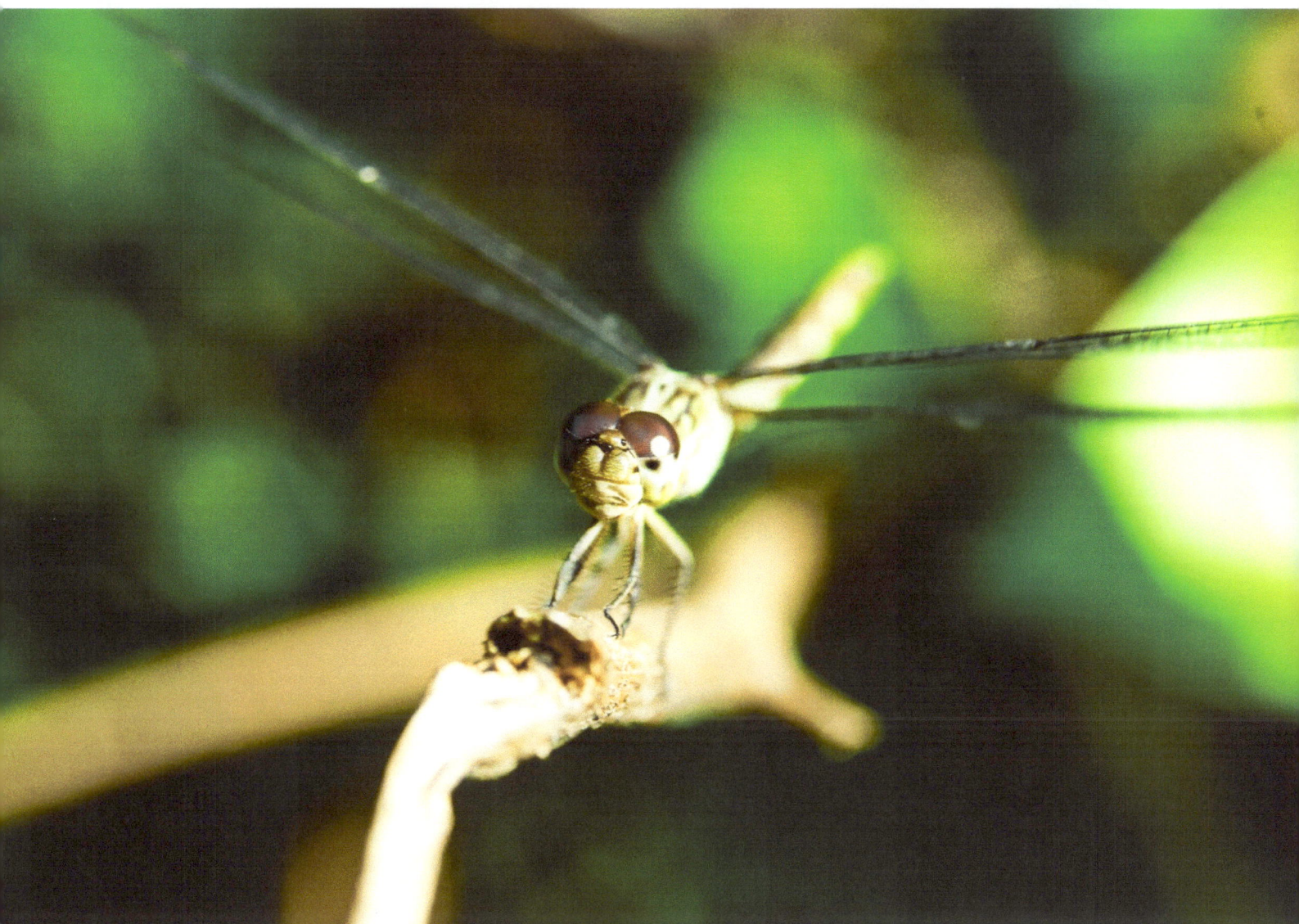

Bandwing Dragonfly
Miami, FL, 2017
Enchanted Forest Elaine Gordon Park

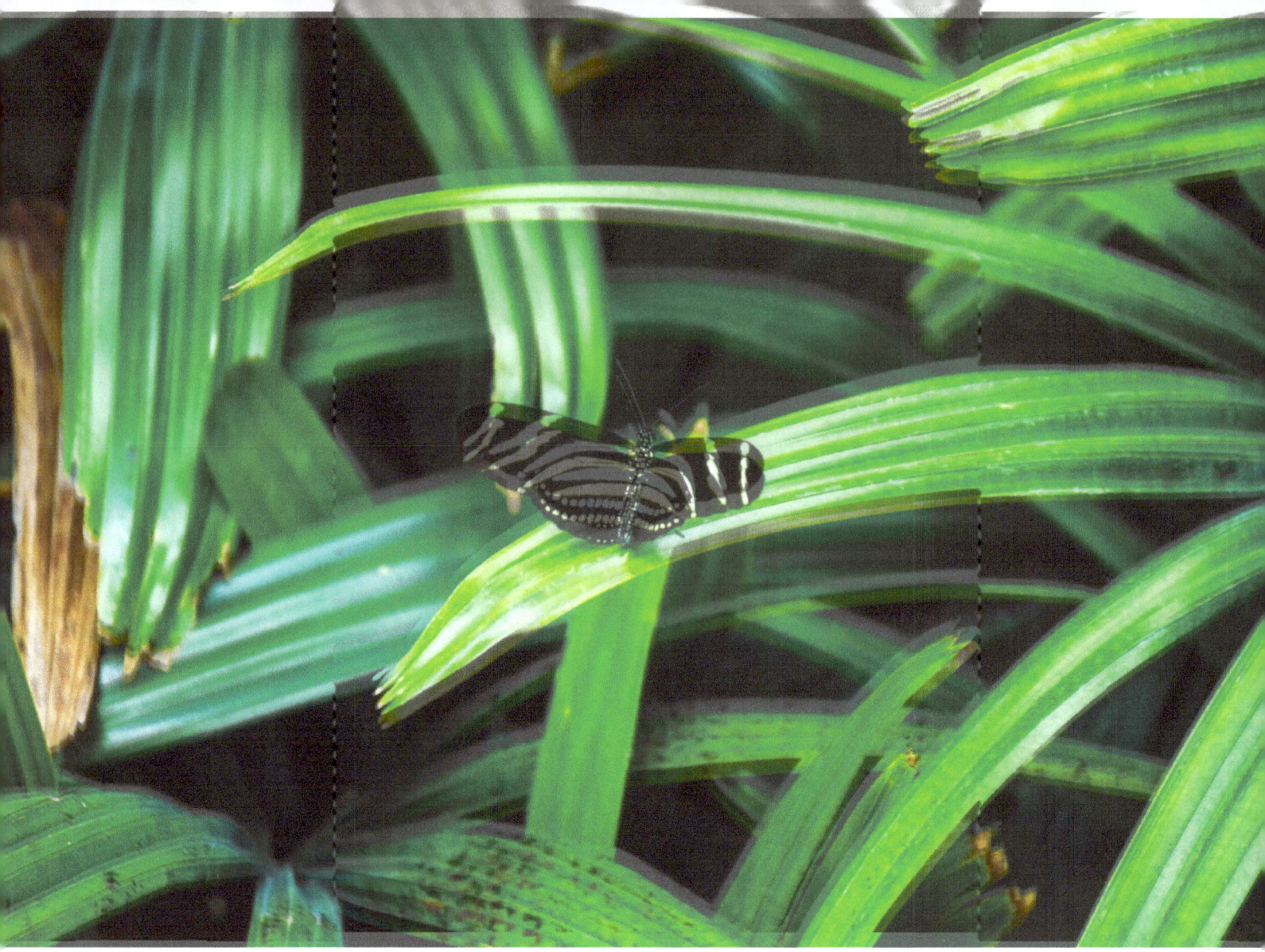

Zebra Longwing Butterfly
Miami, FL; 2017
Miami Beach Botanical Garden

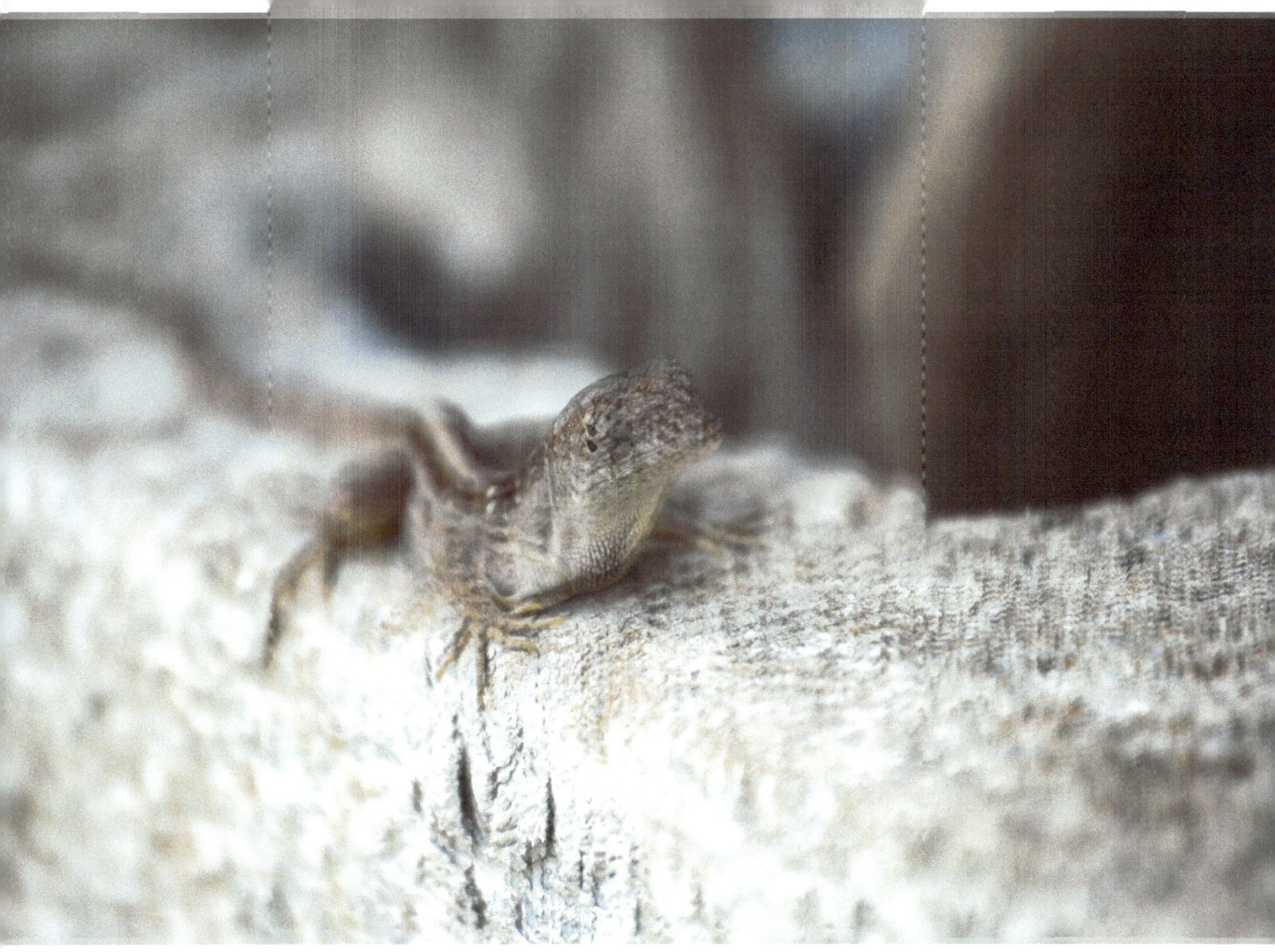

Garden Lizard
Miami, FL; 2017

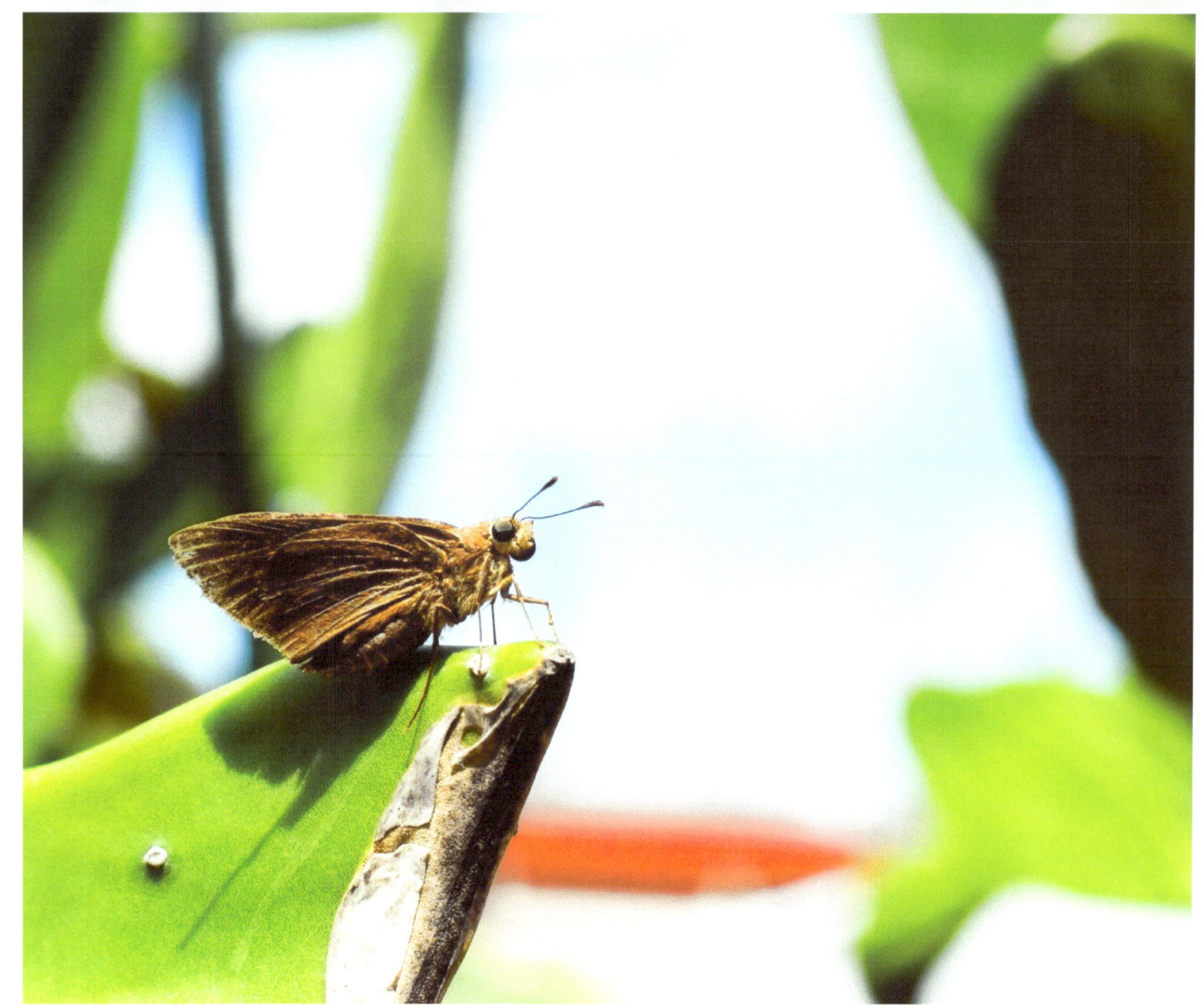

Skipper Butterfly
Miami, FL, 2017

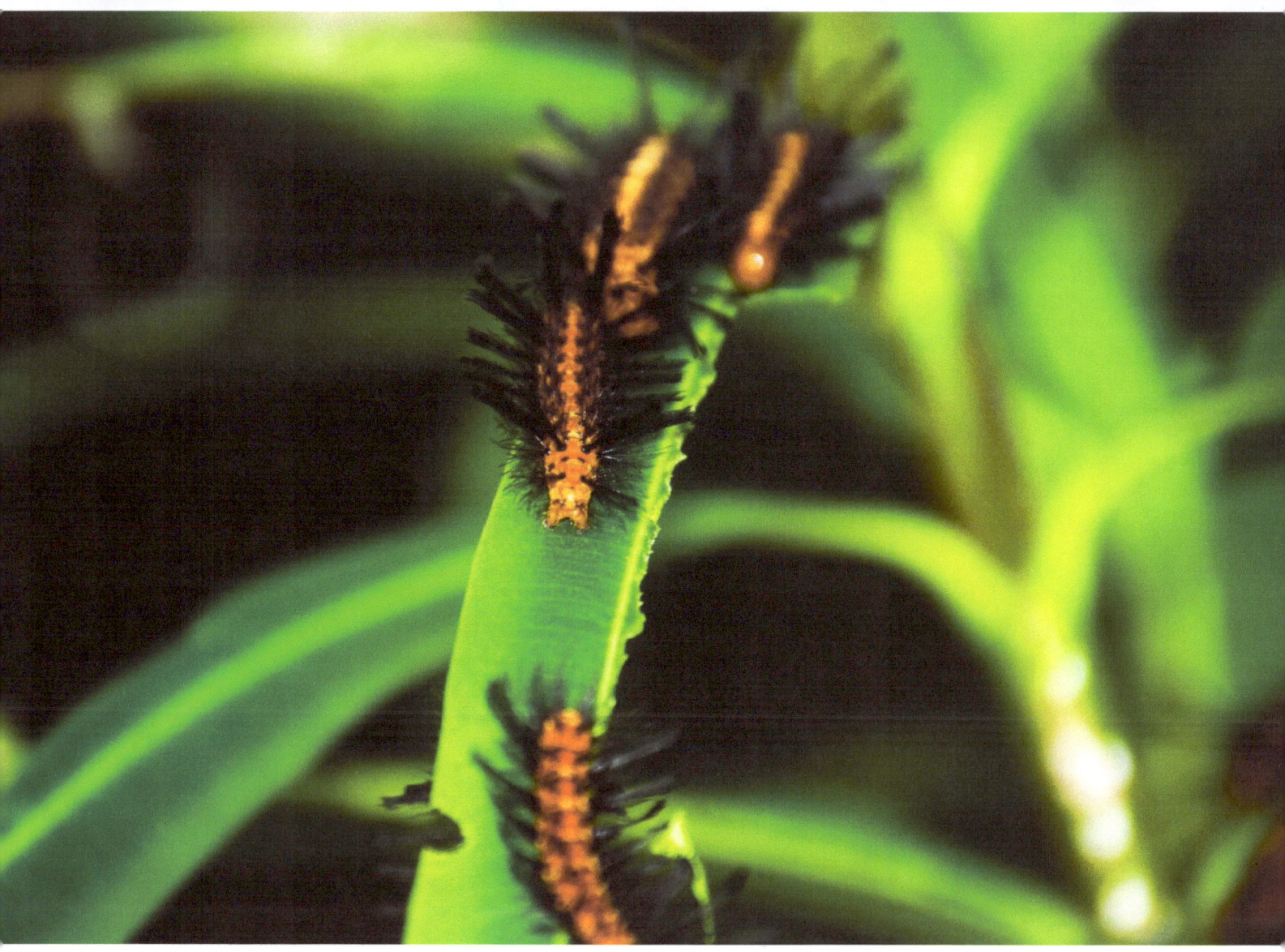

Oleander Caterpillar

Miami, FL, 2017

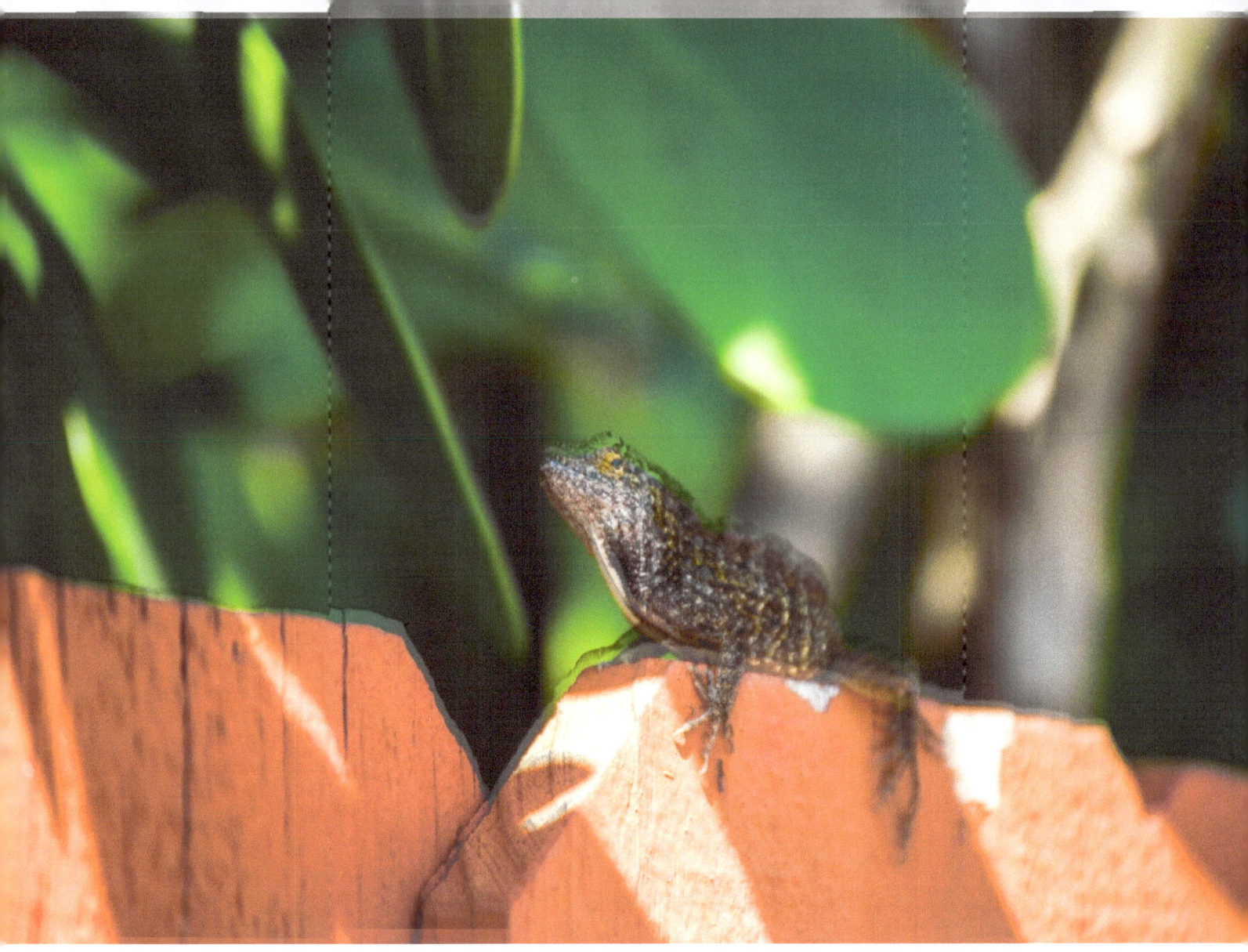

Anole Lizard
Miami, FL; 2017

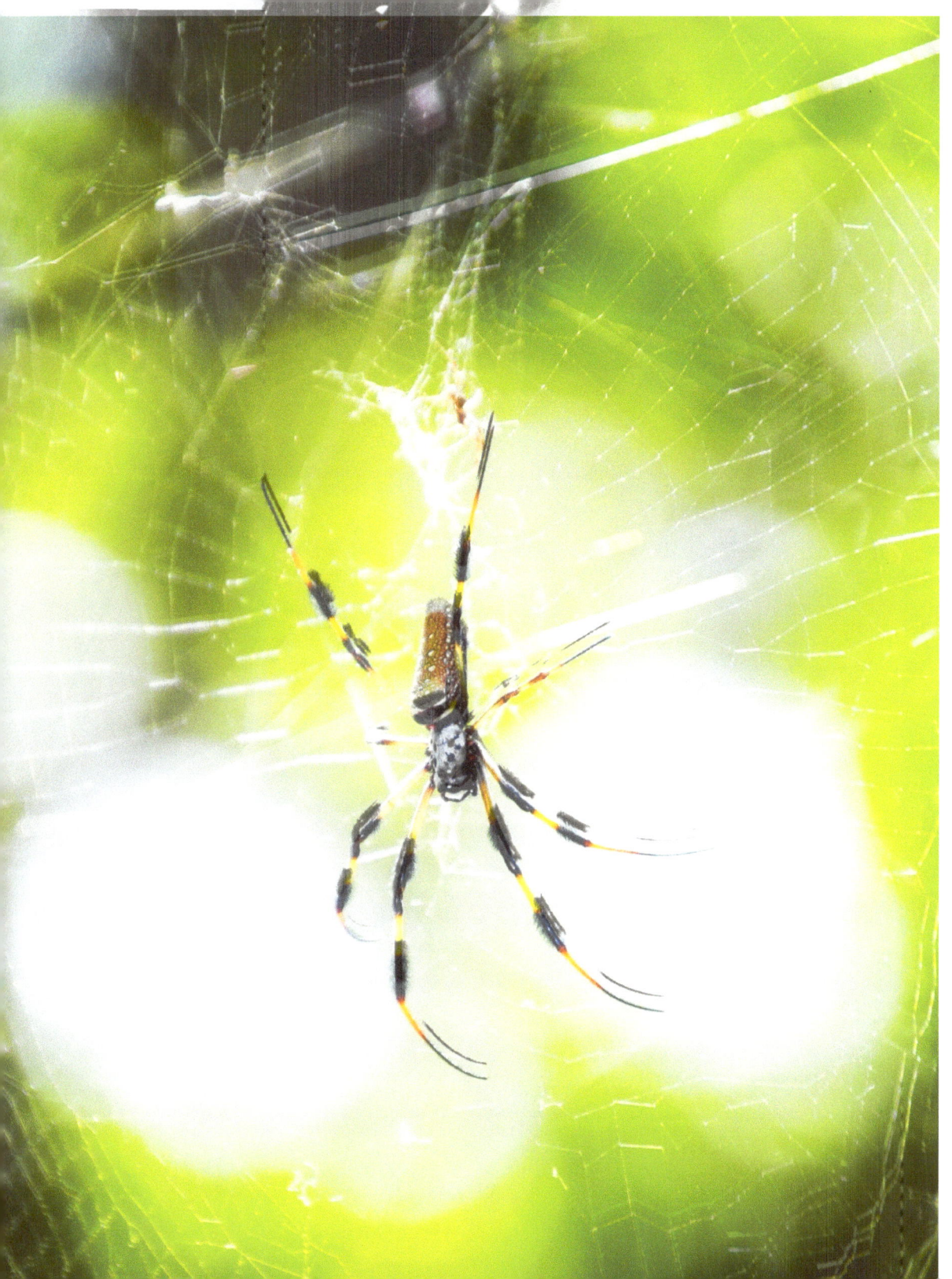

Golden Silk Spider
Miami, FL;
2017
Enchanted Forest Elaine Gordon Park

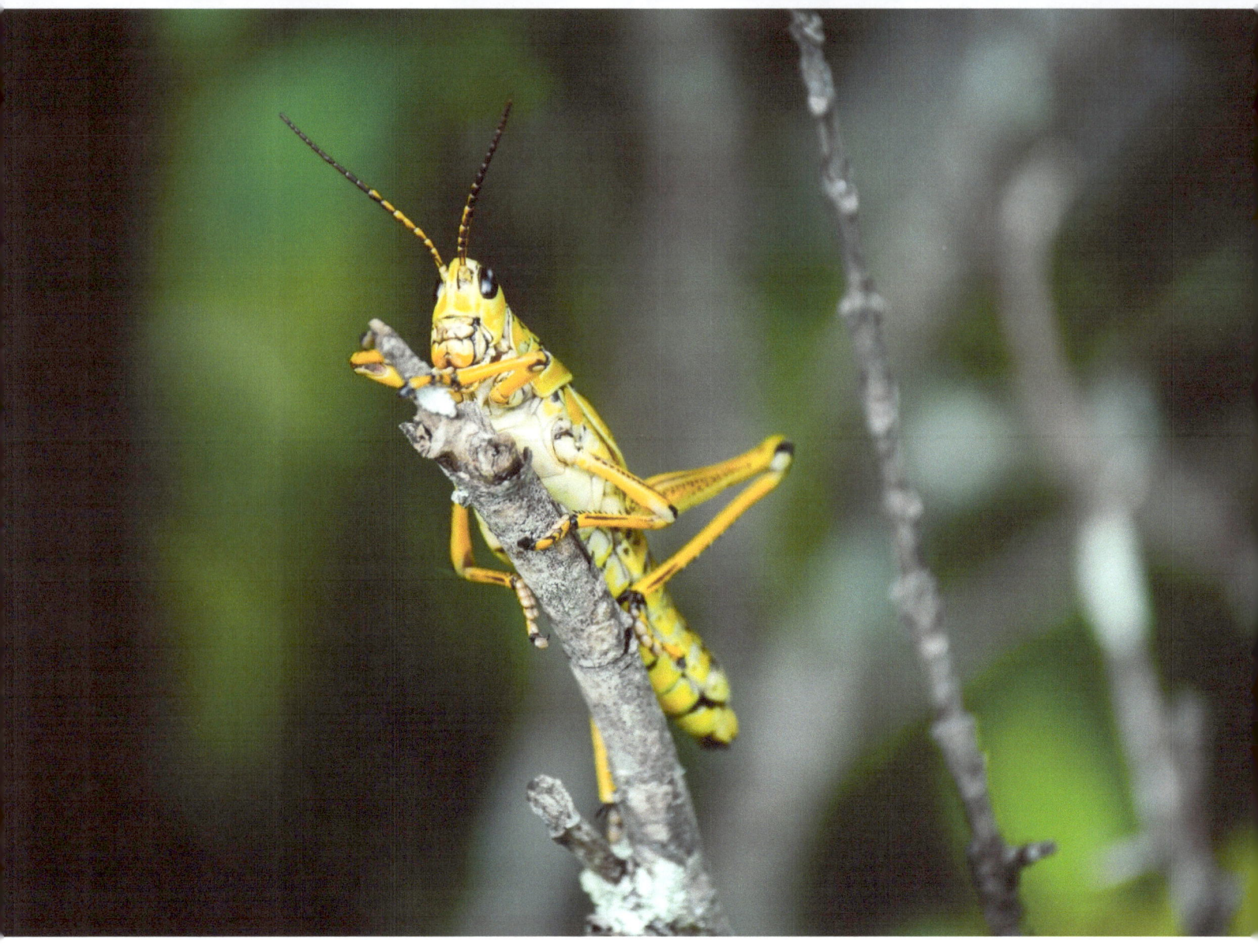

Lubber Grasshopper

Miami, FL, 2017

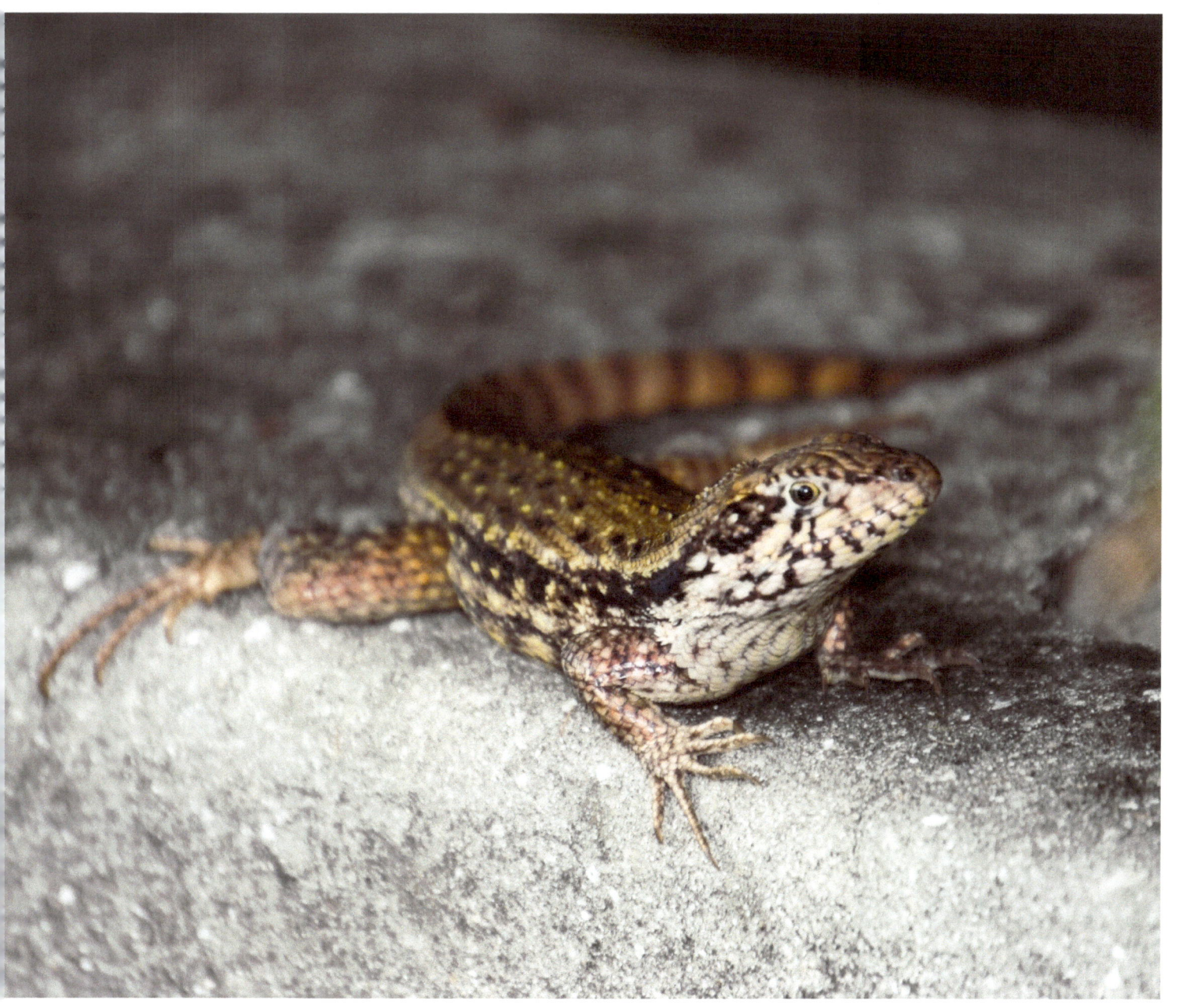

Curly Tail Lizard

Miami, FL, 2017

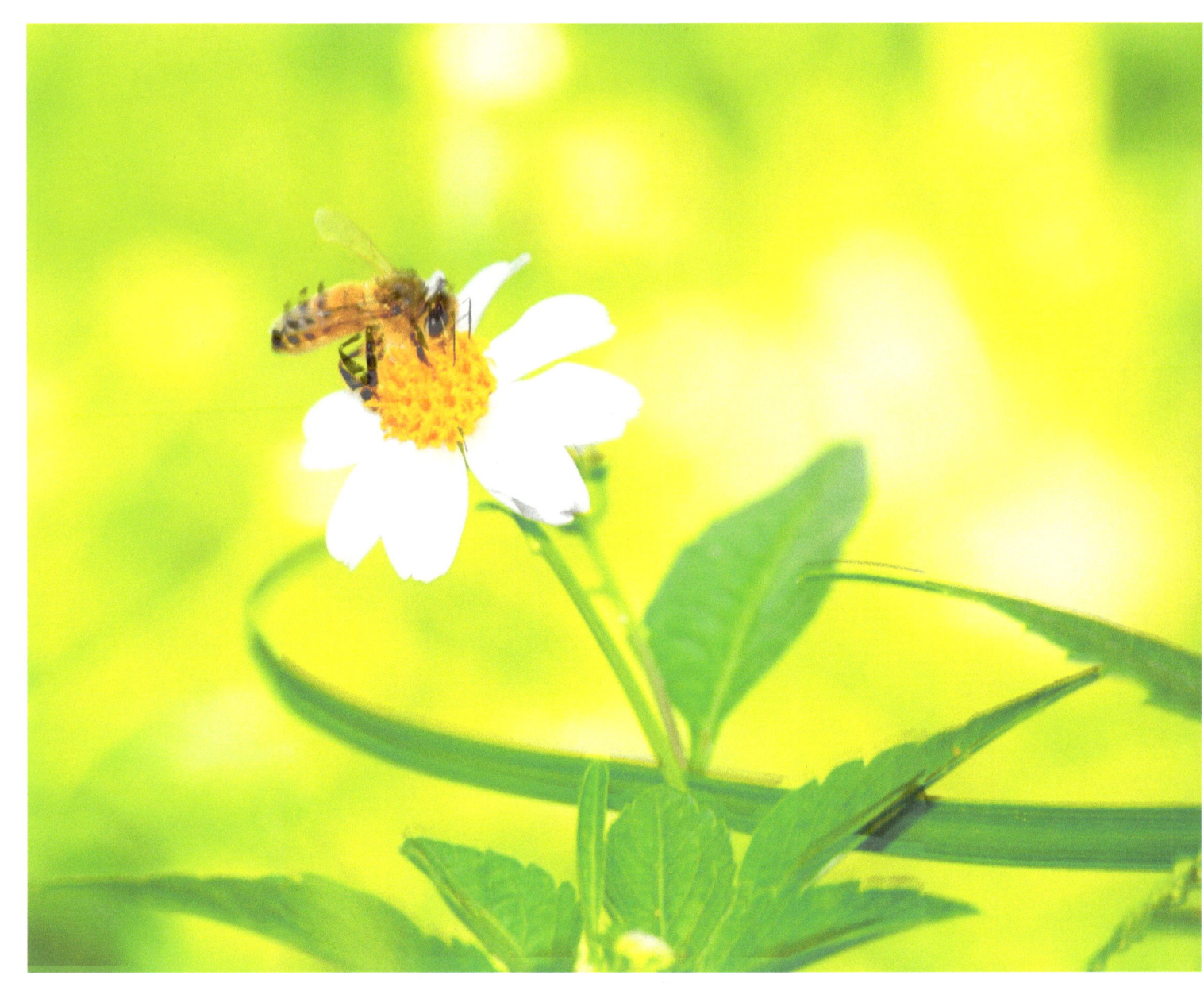

Honeybee
Miami, FL; 2017

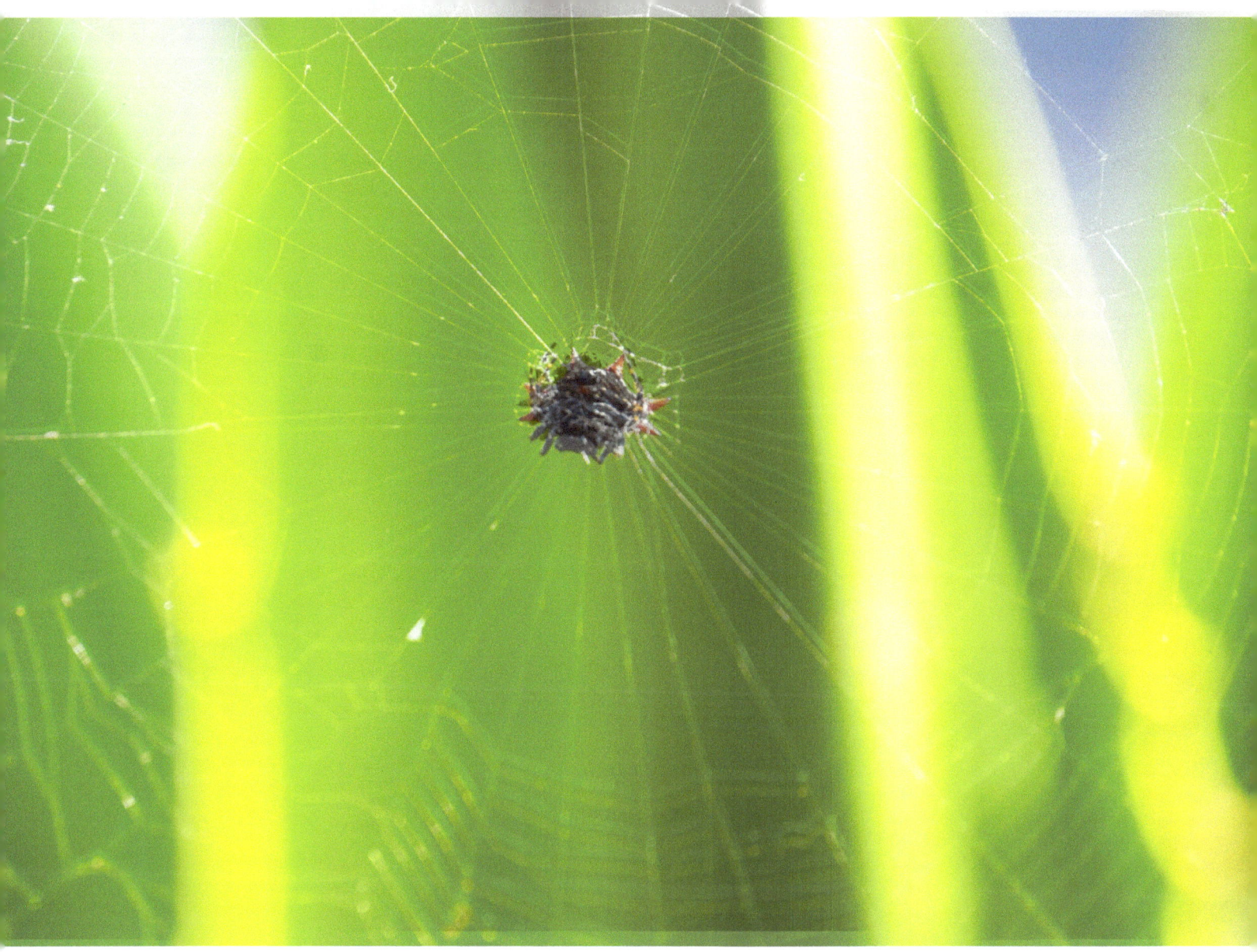

Crab Spider
Miami, FL; 2017

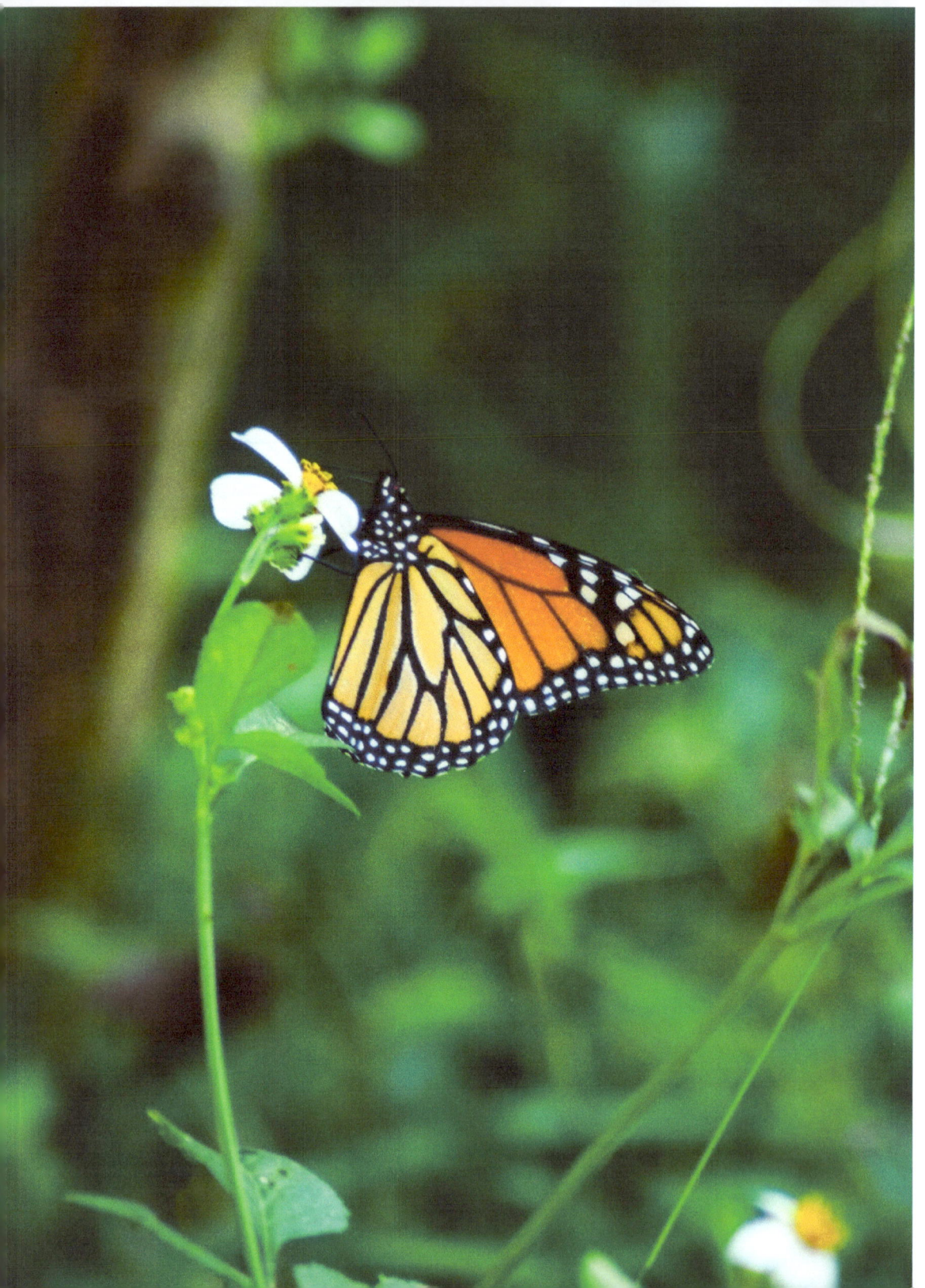

Monarch Butterfly
Miami, FL 2017
Enchanted Forest
Elaine Gordon Park

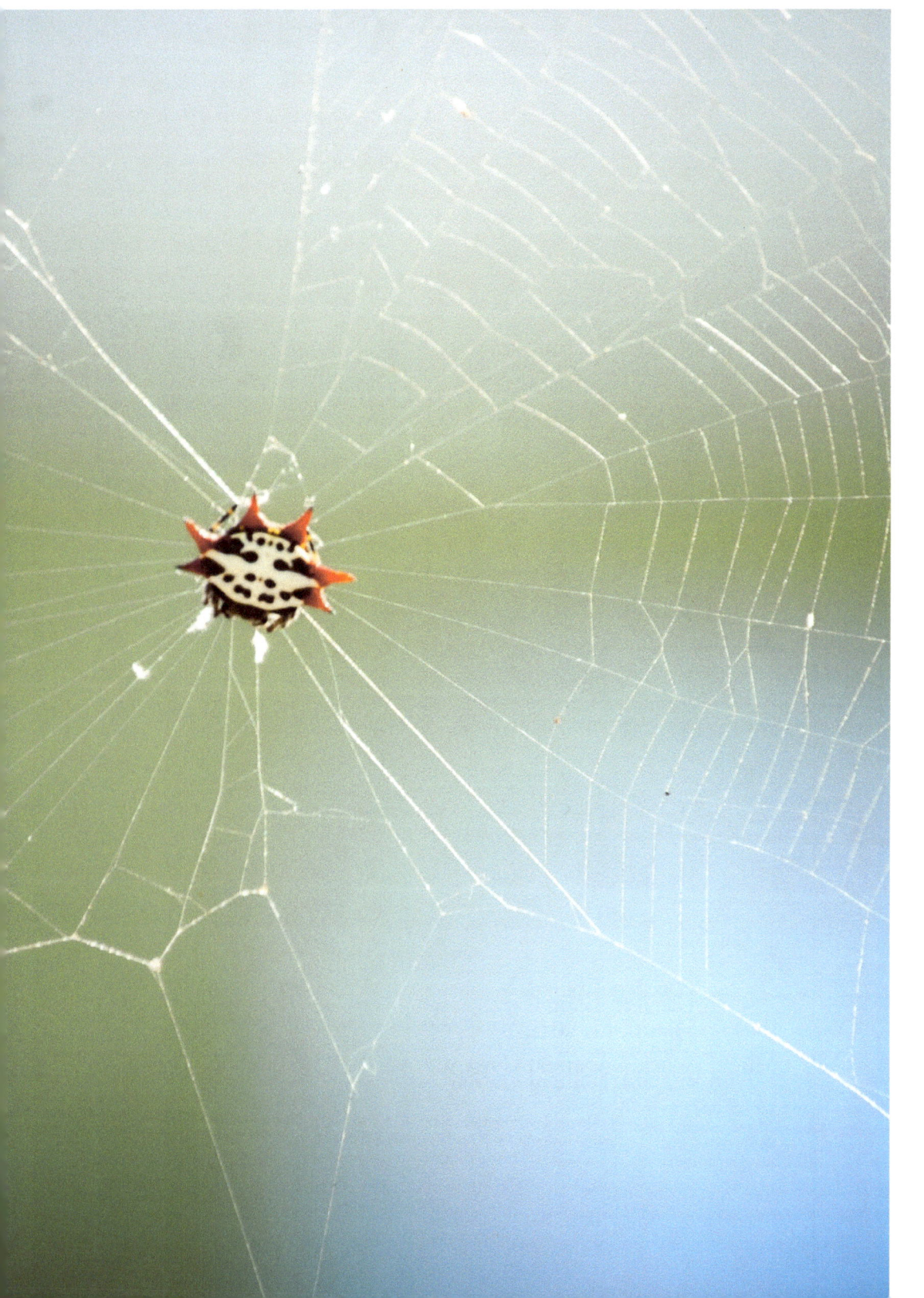

Crab Spider
Miami, FL 2017

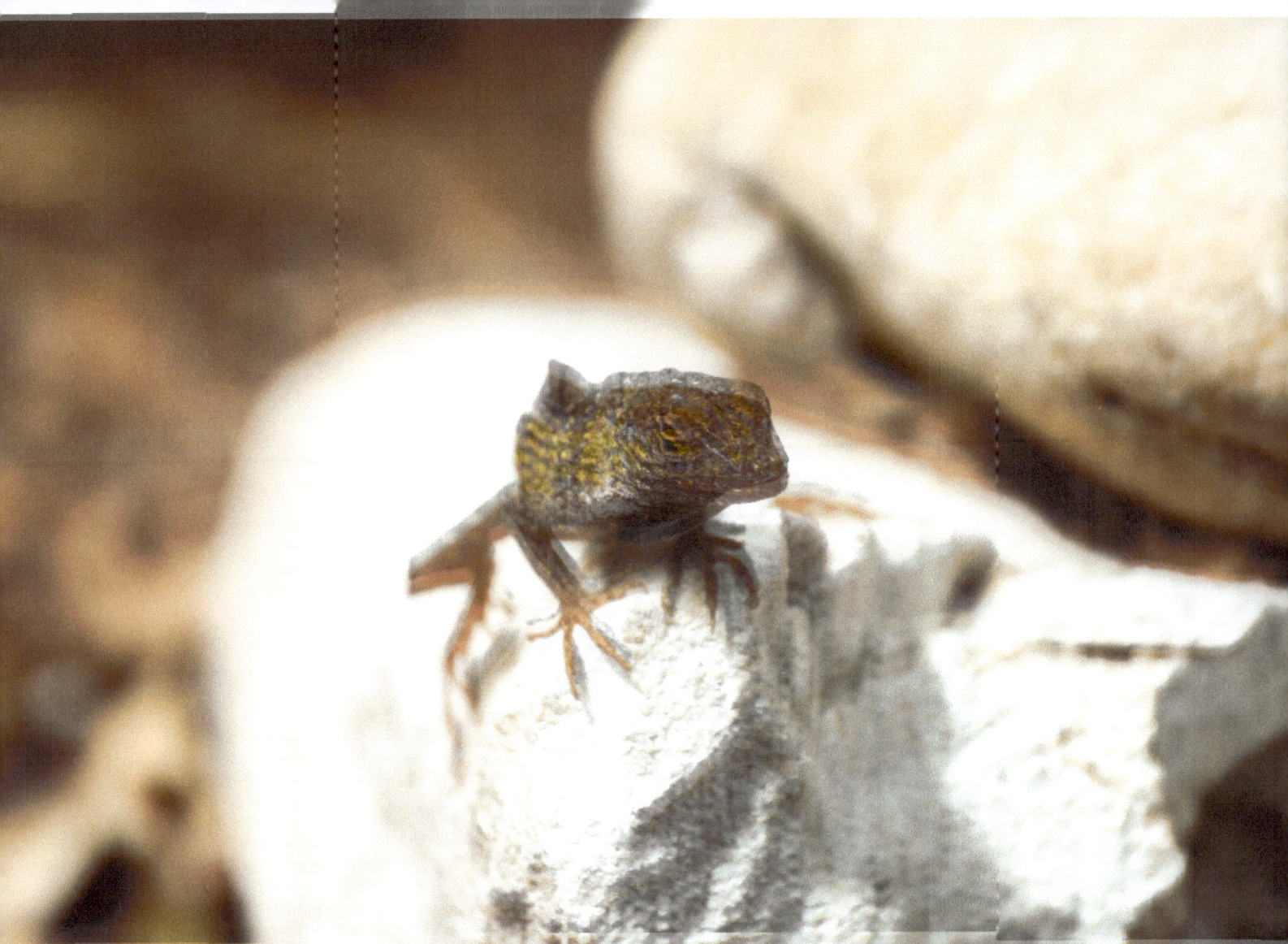

Garden Lizard
Miami, FL 2017
Miami Beach Botanical Garden

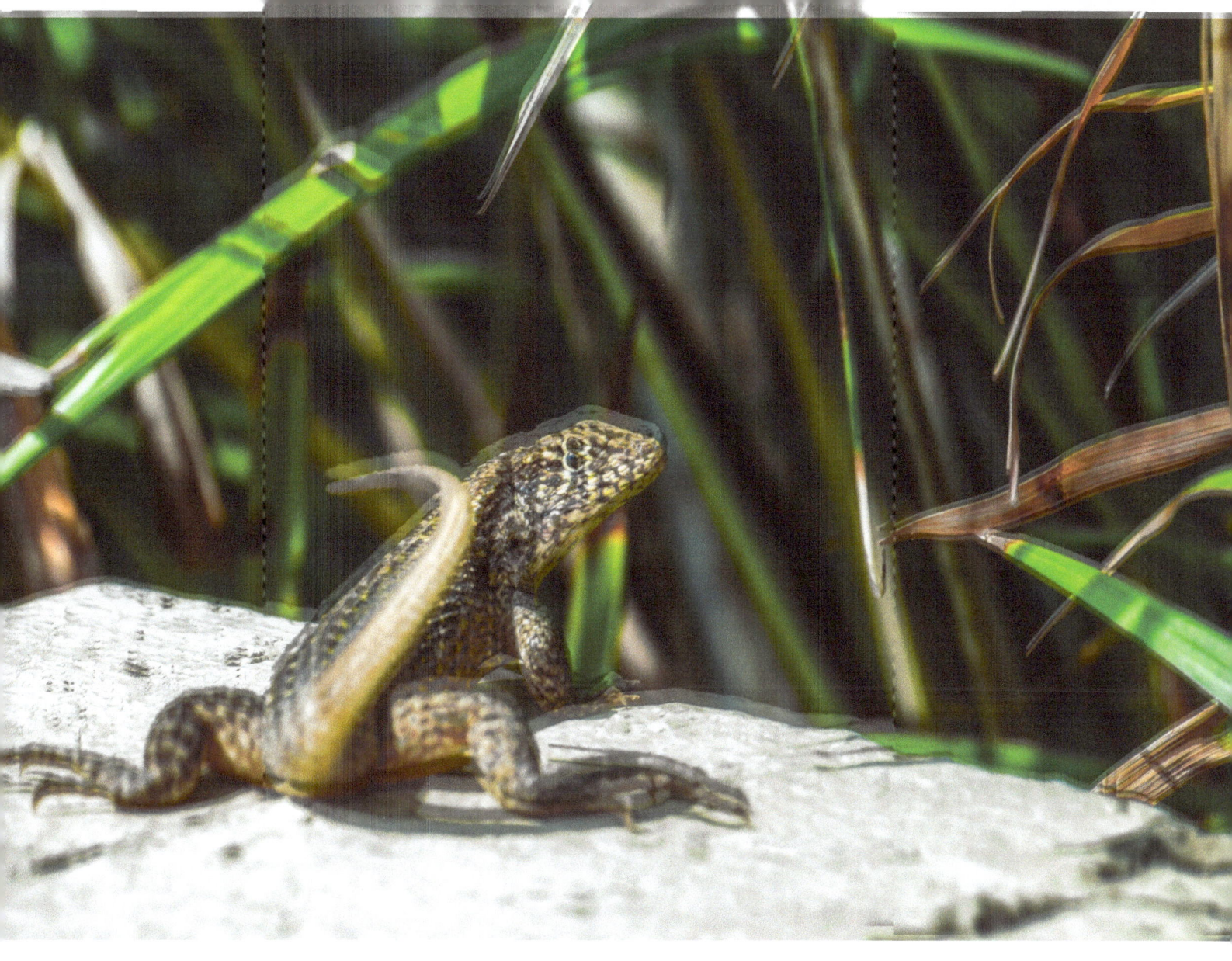

Curly tailed Lizard
Miami, FL

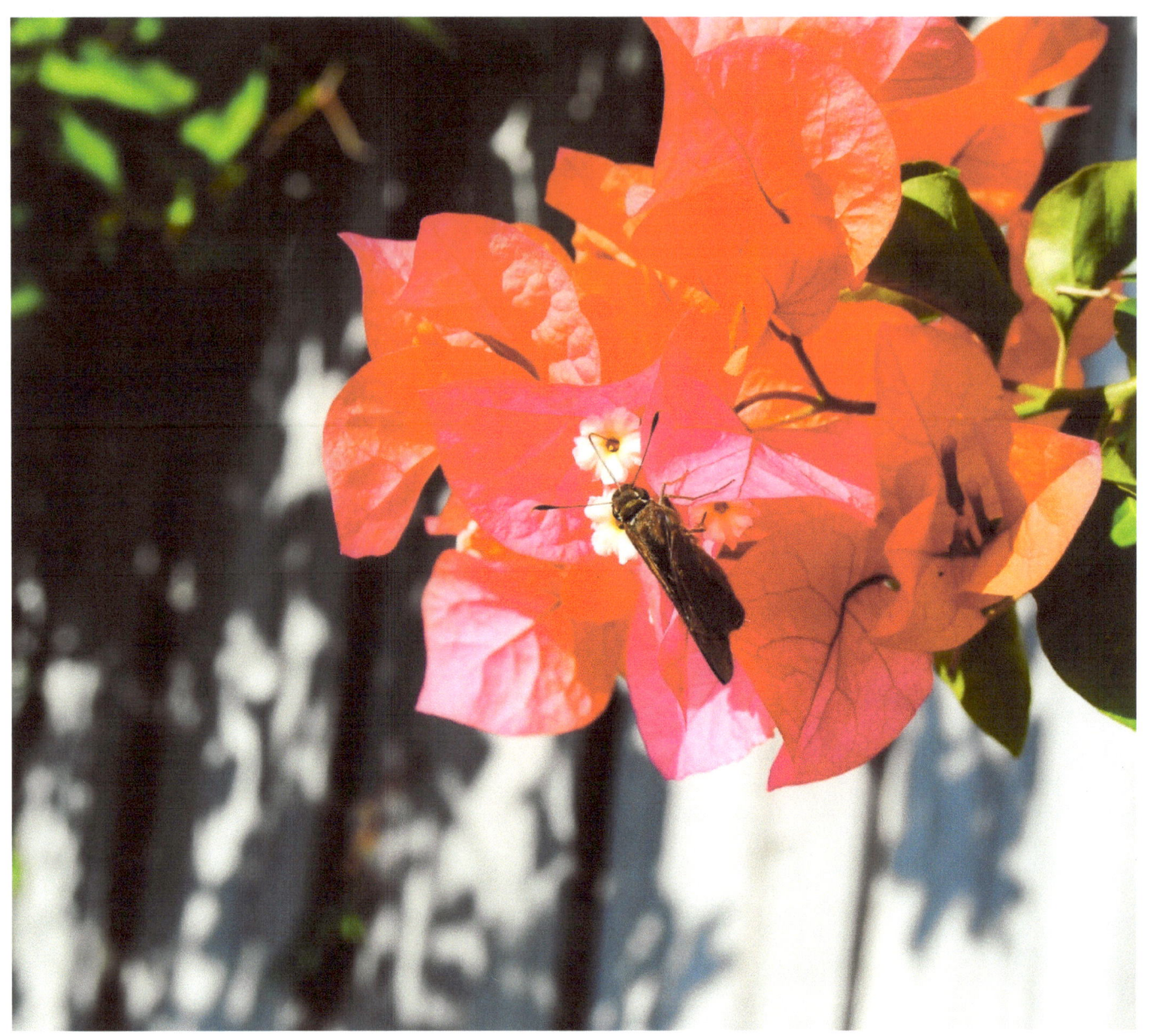

Skipper Butterfly
Miami, FL, 2017

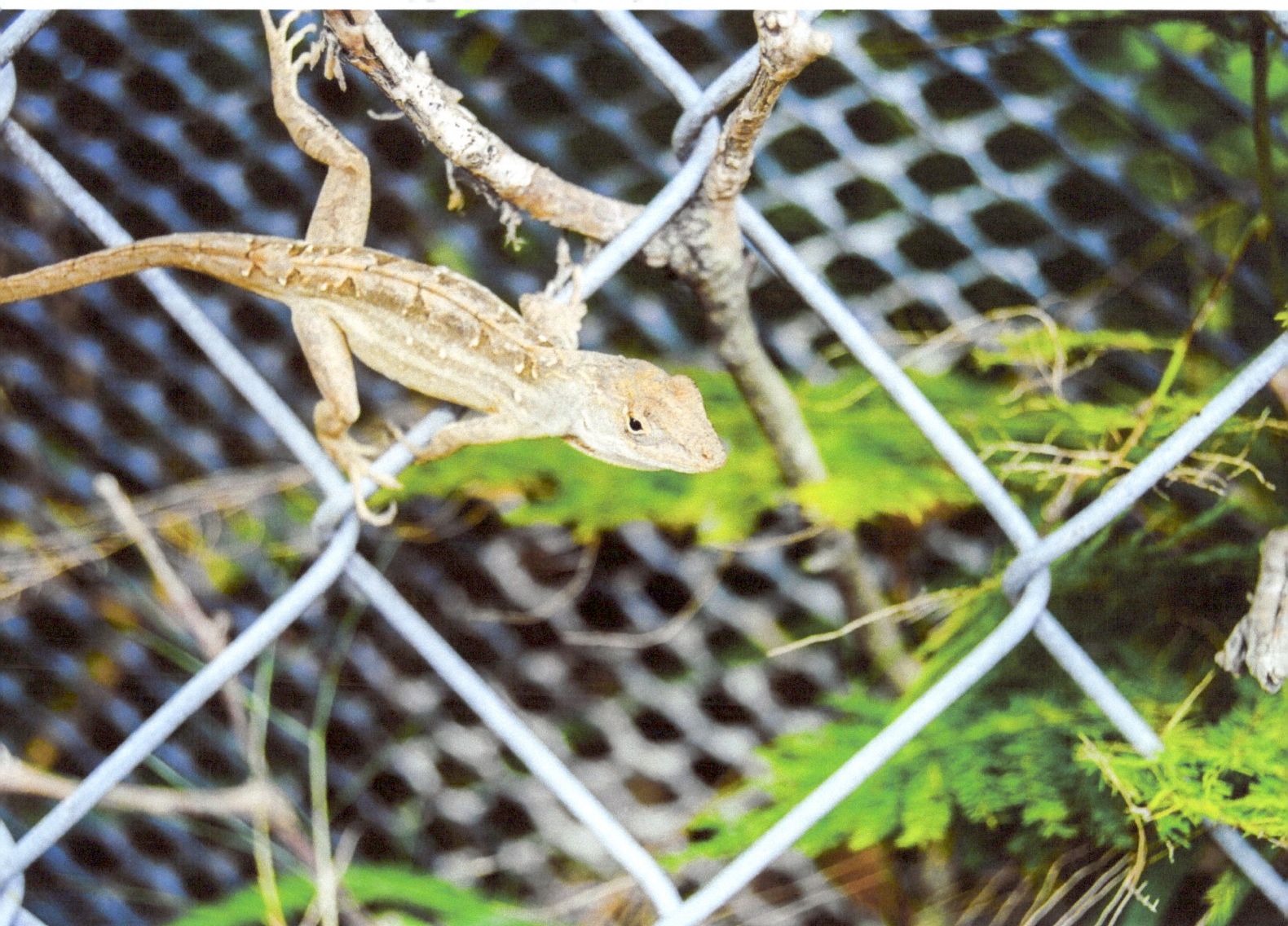

Brown Anole Lizard

Miami, FL 2017

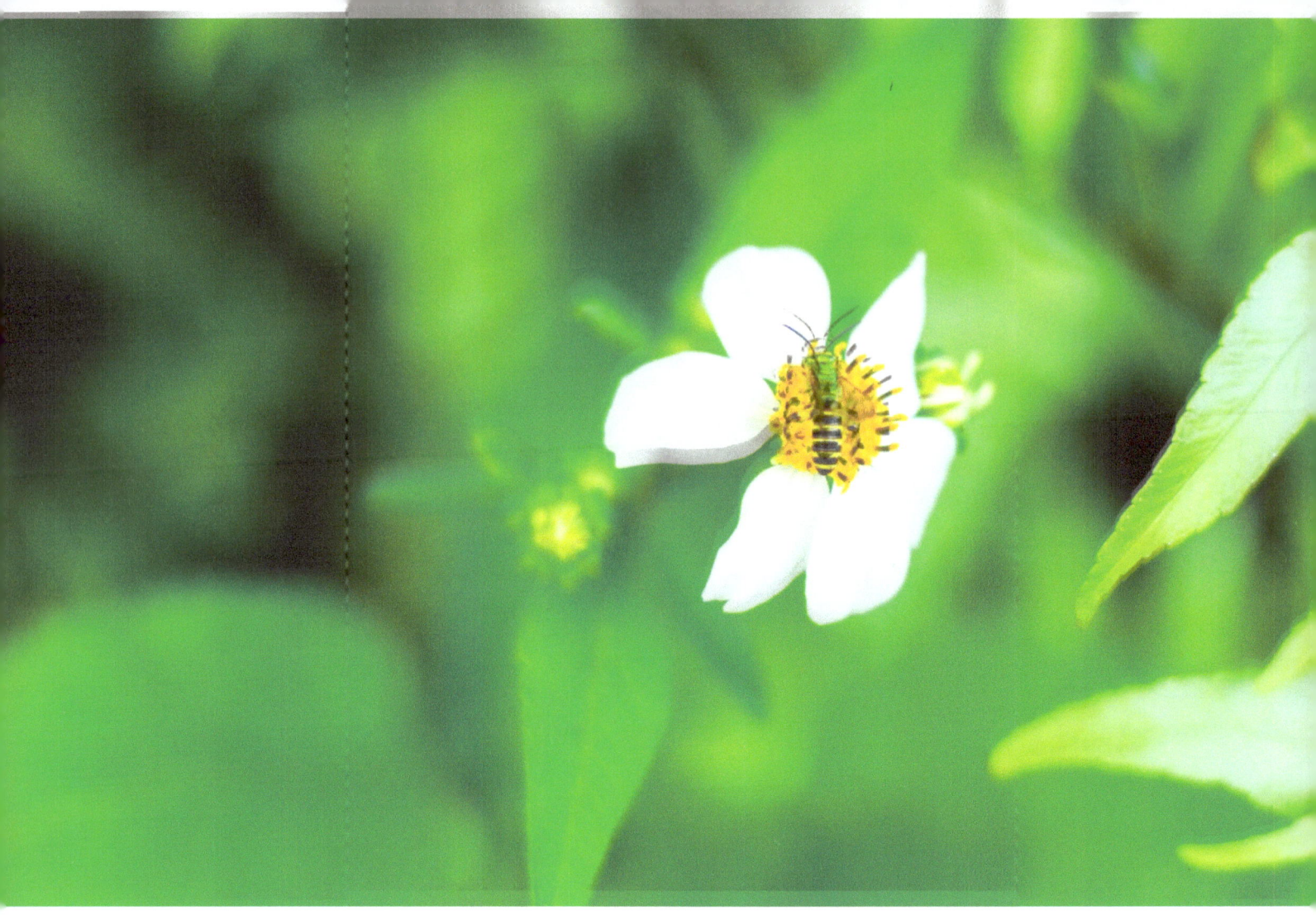

Hoverfly
Miami, FL 2017

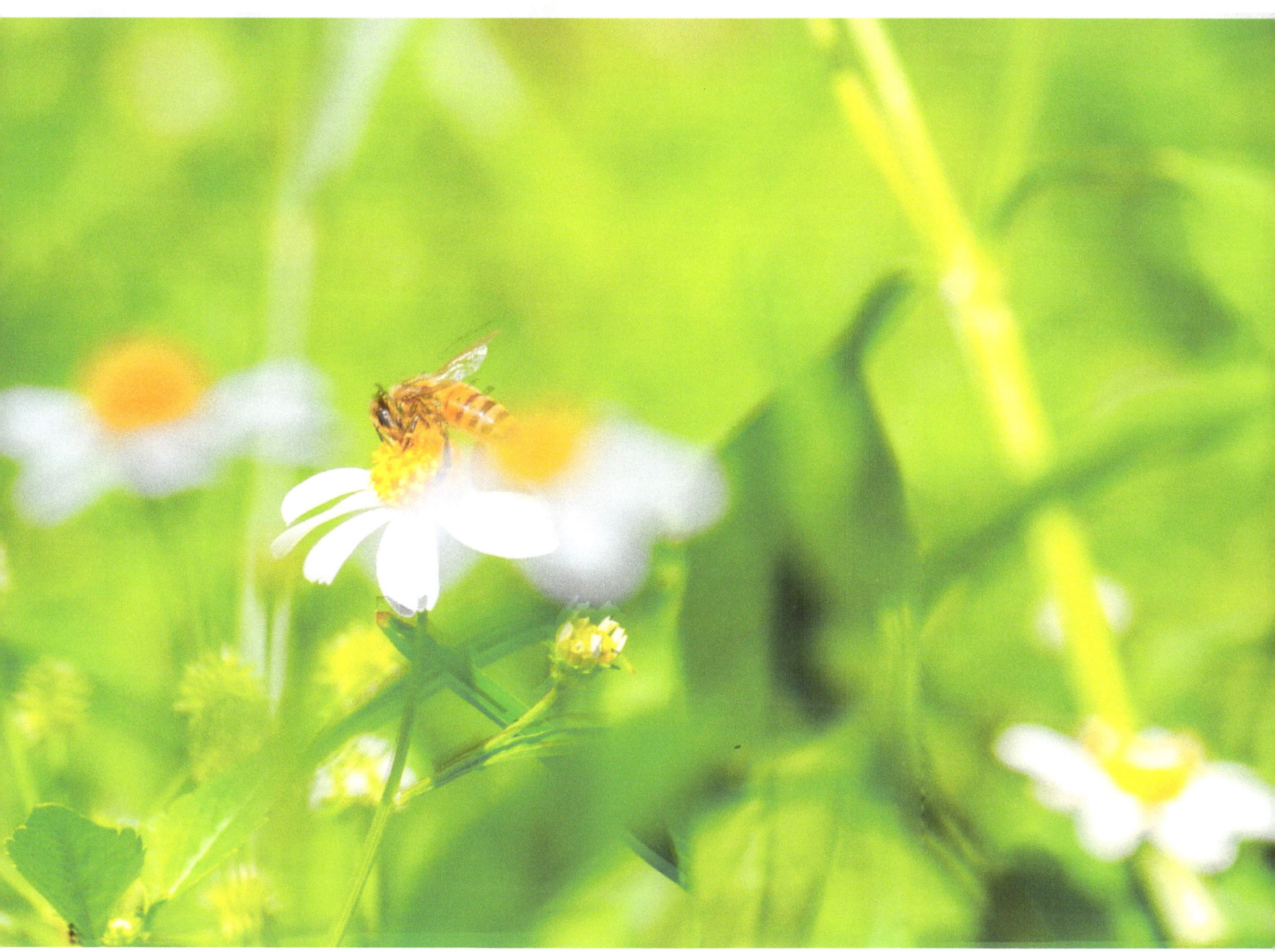

Honeybee
Miami, FL; 2017

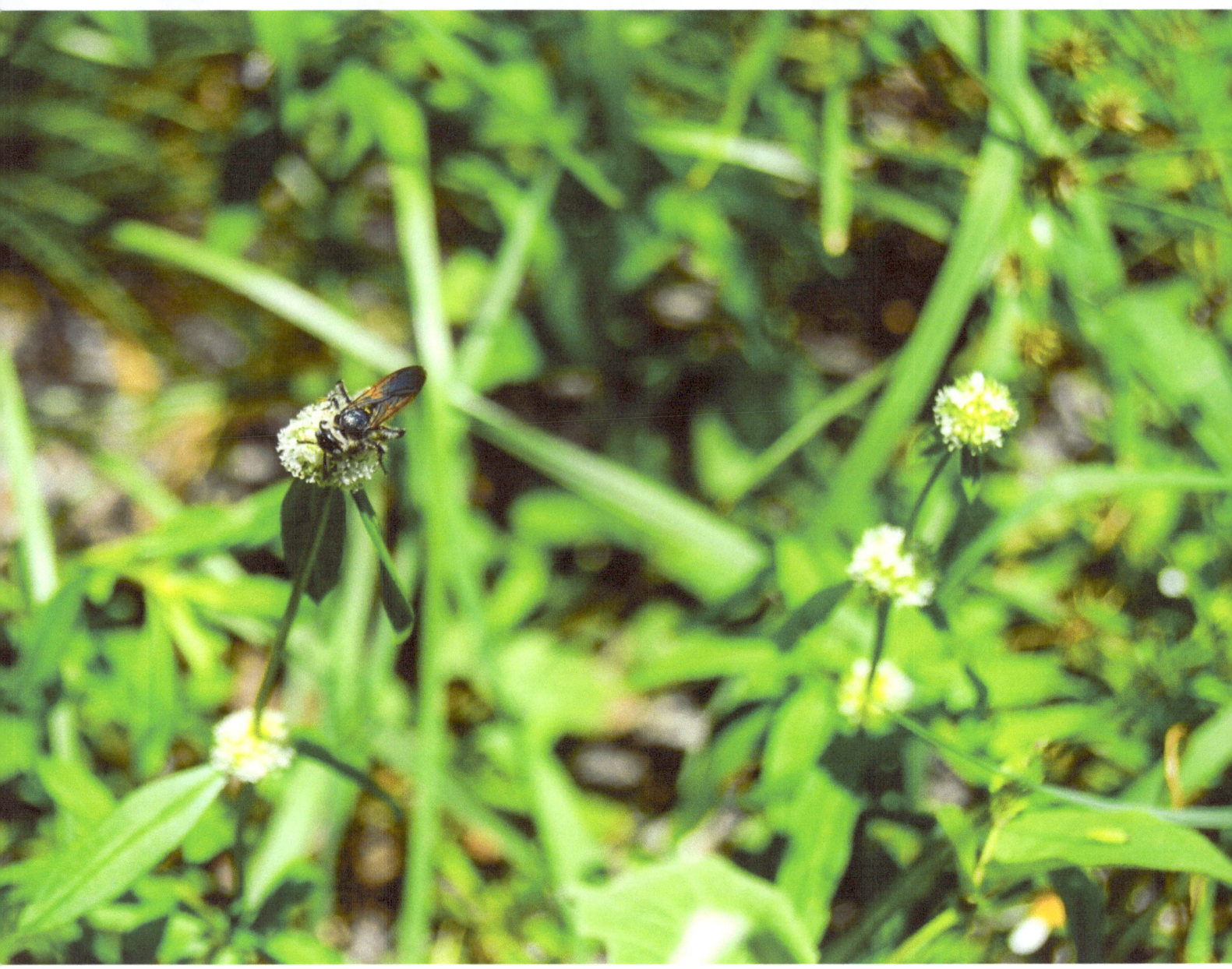

Blow Fly

Miami, FL 2017

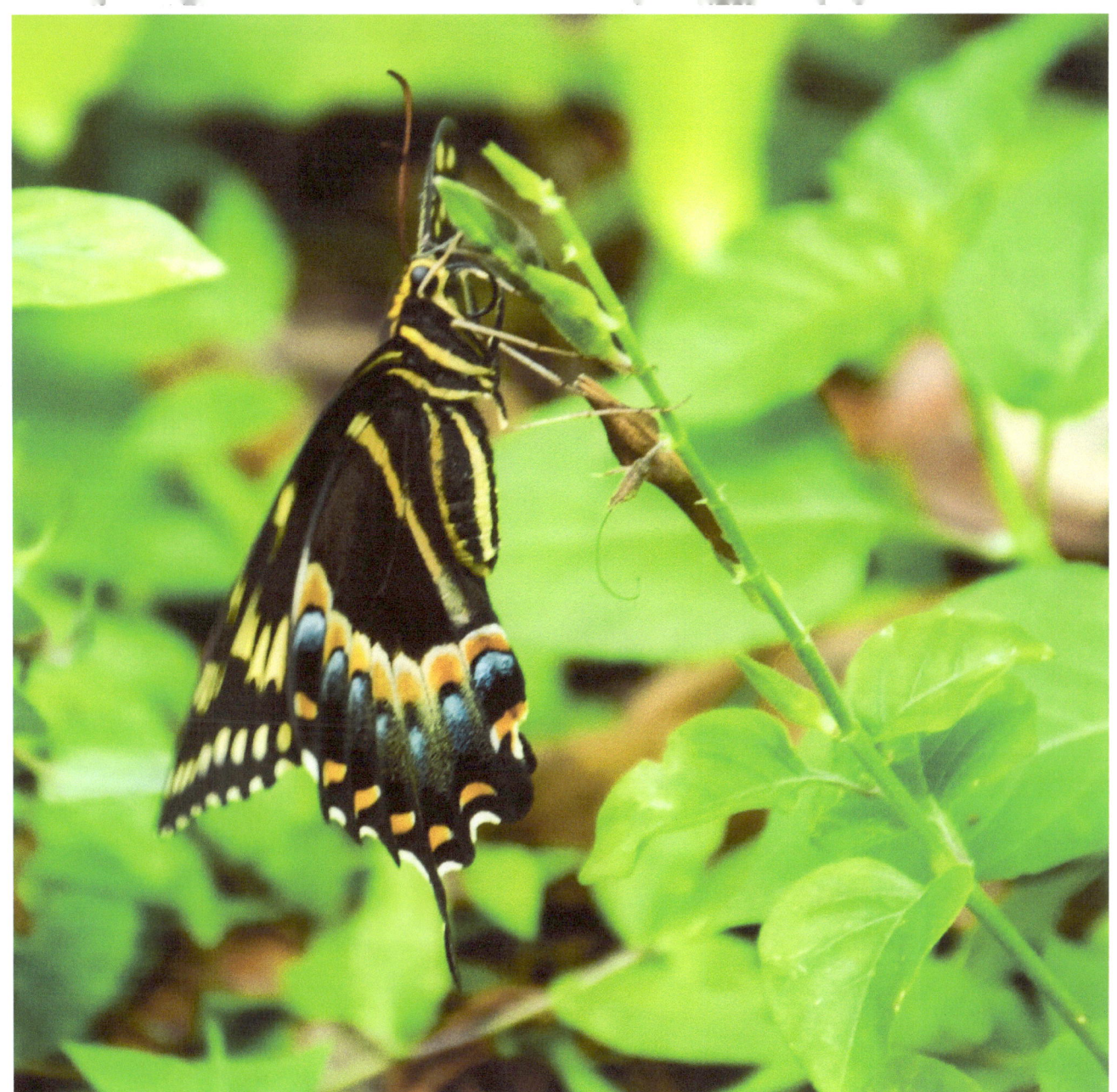

Giant Swallowtail

Miami, FL 2017

About the Author

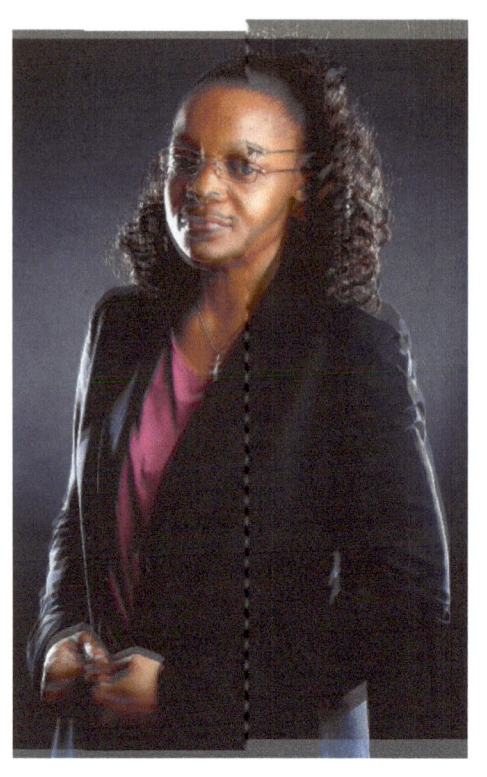

Joanne Guillard is a photographer, writer, and poet. She was born and raised in Miami, Fl. Joanne started writing since the age of 12 and continued learning more about her craft. She is a graduate of Miami Dade College earning an Associate in Science and Barry University earning a Bachelors in Fine Arts, both in Photography. Through her faith she writes about important issues and is a founder of Joanne G Portraits.

www.ingramcontent.com/pod-product-compliance
Lightning Source LLC
Chambersburg PA
CBHW051930210526
45473CB00006B/2197